Horned Dinosaurs

Titles in THE DINOSAUR LIBRARY Series

Armored, Plated, and Bone-Headed Dinosaurs
The Ankylosaurs, Stegosaurs, and Pachycephalosaurs
ISBN 0-7660-1453-3

Feathered Dinosaurs
The Origin of Birds
ISBN 0-7660-1454-1

Gigantic Long-Necked Plant-Eating Dinosaurs
The Prosauropods and Sauropods
ISBN 0-7660-1449-5

Horned Dinosaurs
The Ceratopsians
ISBN 0-7660-1451-7

Meat-Eating Dinosaurs
The Theropods
ISBN 0-7660-1452-5

Peaceful Plant-Eating Dinosaurs
The Iguanodonts, Duckbills, and Other Ornithopods
ISBN 0-7660-1450-9

THE DINOSAUR LIBRARY

Horned Dinosaurs
The Ceratopsians

Thom Holmes and Laurie Holmes

Illustrated by Michael William Skrepnick

Series Advisor:
Dr. Peter Dodson
Professor of Veterinary Anatomy and Paleontology,
University of Pennsylvania
and
co-editor of *The Dinosauria*,
the leading reference used by dinosaur scientists

Enslow Publishers, Inc.

40 Industrial Road	PO Box 38
Box 398	Aldershot
Berkeley Heights, NJ 07922	Hants GU12 6BP
USA	UK

http://www.enslow.com

Library of Congress Cataloging-in-Publication Data

Holmes, Thom.
    Horned dinosaurs : the ceratopsians / Thom Holmes and Laurie Holmes ;
    illustrated by Michael William Skrepnick.
        p. cm. — (The dinosaur library)
    Includes bibliographical references (p.   ) and index.
    ISBN 0-7660-1451-7
    1. Ceratopsidae-Juvenile literature. [1. Ceratopsians. 2. Dinosaurs.] I. Holmes,
Laurie. II. Skrepnick, Michael William, ill. III. Title. IV. Dinosaur library (Berkeley
Heights, N.J.)
    QE862.O65 H65 2001
    567.915—dc21
                                  00-010018

Printed in the United States of America

10 9 8 7 6 5 4 3 2 1

To Our Readers: We have done our best to make sure all Internet Addresses in this book were
active and appropriate when we went to press. However, the author and the publisher have
no control over and assume no liability for the material available on those Internet sites or on
other Web sites they may link to. Any comments or suggestions can be sent by e-mail to
comments@enslow.com or to the address on the back cover.

CONTENTS

About the Authors 6

About the Illustrator 7

Dangerous River 9

1 Dinosaurs Defined 17

2 Origins and Evolution 27

3 Geographic Range 35

4 Anatomy 41

5 Physiology 63

6 Eggs and Babies 75

7 Feeding Habits and Adaptations 79

8 Ceratopsian Defenses 85

9 Extinction of the Dinosaurs 93

10 Major Discoveries
    of Horned Dinosaurs 97

Currently Known Horned Dinosaurs . . .107

Chapter Notes 109

Glossary 114

Further Reading 119

Internet Addresses 123

Index 125

ABOUT THE AUTHORS

Thom Holmes is a natural history writer specializing in dinosaur science. He has dug for dinosaurs with leading paleontologists in the United States and South America. He has collaborated with Dr. Peter Dodson on several dinosaur-related projects during the past fifteen years.

Laurie Holmes is a science writer and editor, as well as a reading specialist. It has been her privilege to associate with many of the world's leading dinosaur scientists and artists through her work with her husband, Thom. Originally a teacher, she maintains that she is still teaching by writing and editing books for young adults.

On a dig in Patagonia, Thom Holmes holds part of the skull bone of what is currently known as the largest meat-eating dinosaur ever.

Thom Holmes

Laurie Holmes

AUTHORS' NOTE

Dinosaurs hold a special fascination for people all over the world. In writing *The Dinosaur Library*, we enjoyed sharing the knowledge that allows scientists to understand what dinosaurs were really like. You will learn about the differences that make groups of dinosaurs unique, as well as the many similarities that dinosaurs shared.

The Dinosaur Library covers all the suborders of dinosaurs, from the meat-eating theropods, such as *Tyrannosaurus rex*, to the gigantic plant eaters. We hope you enjoy learning about these fascinating creatures that ruled the earth for 160 million years.

About the Illustrator

Michael William Skrepnick is an established paleo artist with a lifelong interest in dinosaurs. He has worked on newly described dinosaurs with a number of the world's leading paleontologists. His original artworks are found in a number of art collections and reproduced as museum murals, and in popular books, magazines, scientific journals, and television documentaries.
Michael lives and works in Alberta, Canada, close to some of the richest Upper Cretaceous dinosaur fossil localities in the world.

Paleo art is a field devoted to the reconstruction and life restoration of long extinct animals and their environments. Since we cannot observe dinosaurs (other than living birds) in nature, we may never truly know their habits, lifestyles, or the color of their skin. In addition, the fossil record provides only a fraction of the remains of a wide diversity of life on earth.

Many fairly complete skeletons of dinosaurs have been unearthed in recent history. Others are represented by as little as a fragment of a single fractured bone, an isolated tooth, or a footprint impressed in once-wet mud. It is still possible to create a reliable portrait of unique, previously unknown creatures, but the accuracy of the art depends on the following:

- The quality and amount of actual skeletal material of the specimen preserved
- Discussion and collaboration with a paleontologist familiar with the fossil material and locality from which it was excavated
- Observation and comparisons to the closest related living forms
- The technical abilities, skill, and disciplined vision of the artist

The resulting artwork can draw the viewer back in time into exotic worlds of the ancient.

DANGEROUS RIVER

*T*he rain in the highlands had been pounding the earth for days. The once parched soil was turning muddy and opened into ever widening crevasses leading down the hills to the valley below. In the valley, a river fed by mountain streams swelled and overflowed its banks with the floodwaters of spring.

Any creature looking down from high in the hills could not have helped noticing a mass of living creatures approaching from the distant horizon. The mass crept over the plain, moving closer and closer to the swollen river that divided the valley before it. It grew larger and spread out wide as it swarmed into the valley. It was a sight seen but once a year in this valley: the annual migration to their nesting grounds of the horned dinosaurs known as centrosaurs. Unfortunately for the enormous herd, their destination lay miles on the other side of the dangerous river rapids.

The herd numbered in the thousands. Male and female centrosaurs, old and young, rambled along, stopping to rest and feed along the way.

Three females, their bony neck frills distinctively smaller than those of the males, trotted away from a group of male suitors that had been shadowing them. The largest and eldest male of the group took pursuit and was immediately joined by one of his young rivals. This caused the elder centrosaur to stop in his tracks and swing around to block the path of the younger male. He stuck his front feet firmly in the mud and stared down his rival, lowering his head slightly so that the full expanse of his elaborate neck frill could be seen. It made him look even bigger than he was and startled the younger male. The elder male stood his ground and shook his head back and forth, waving his nose horn as a challenge.

The young centrosaur paused but sensed that he could outmaneuver his elder by slipping past him. He made a sudden dash to run around him.

The elder male had seen this move before. He quickly turned and stepped into the path of his rival, nose down and horn extended. The younger male collided and locked horns with him, mostly by accident, then backed off. They faced off, grunting and staring each other down, shuffling their feet, shaking their frills, waiting for the other to stand aside and give up. But neither would yield. Finally the younger male lost patience and found the nerve to step forward with a sudden rush. The two locked nose horns again. Pressing against each other, engaging their horns like two people would use their hands in a game of arm wrestling, they pressed against one another until the younger centrosaur was overpowered and shoved aside. That was the end of the contest. The elder male stood his ground for a moment to see if any other young bulls would challenge him, but none did. His attention returned to the pursuit of the females, who had now blended into the moving mass of the herd.

Yearling centrosaurs, hatched after last year's migration, dashed about playfully among a forest of adult centrosaur legs. Their nose horns were barely noticeable at this young age, a mere bump between the nostrils. Their frills, too, were small and barely formed. The frills and horns would become more prominent as the centrosaurs grew older. The juvenile males and females were sprouting horns and decorative frills quite rapidly. Some of them still seemed unaccustomed to the weight and changing shape of their heads. They rubbed their frills against one another in play, knocking and bumping with the small spikes and bony knobs that adorned them. Their nose horns, nearly fully grown, were useful for shaking the branches of bushes and pulling up ground cover along with clumps of mud and dirt.

It took several hours for the entire herd to enter the valley. The river was like a wall that prevented them from going any farther. Instinct compelled them to move on, however. Soon the centrosaurs found themselves crowded near the edge of the river at a point that had once been a safe place at which to cross. The thousands of animals waited impatiently for the crossing to begin. Those in the rear of the herd were too far away to know the danger that the swift-running water posed. They shoved forward, unknowingly edging those in front of them closer and closer to the river.

The herd was led by several bull males gathered at the crossing point. The water rushed by with great fury, overflowing the banks of the normally calm waterway. An eerie cloud of water

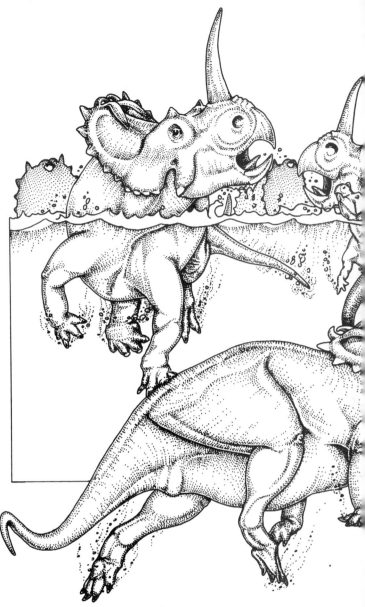

vapor rose above the crushing current, making it difficult for the animals to see the other side of the river. The leaders of the herd instinctively knew that there was no stopping the crossing. When one of them made the leap to cross, the others would begin to follow.

The first centrosaur to jump into the river was swept under almost immediately. It had leaped into a deep spot. Only its nose

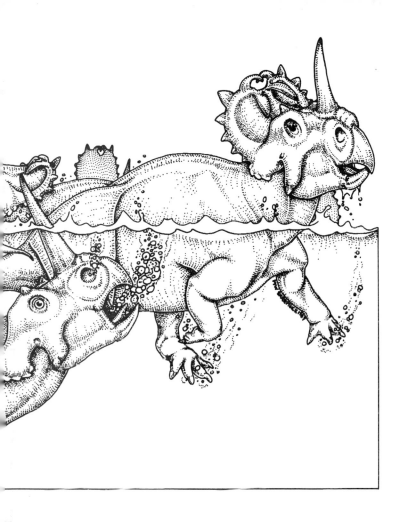

horn was visible as the three-ton beast sank and was dragged away, drowning as it mingled with the limbs of trees and other debris that rushed along with the current. The other centrosaurs paid no heed to this attempt.

The second bull to try to cross the river was luckier. It leaped at a spot where its feet could touch the rocks and mud of the riverbed. Its head bobbed as it began to swim for the other side. He swung his tail back and forth to steer himself straight. Rushing water splashed against his neck frill, sending a cloud of water up around his head. The strong male struggled but continued without *being swept away. By the time he reached midstream, other centrosaurs were beginning to follow.*

One by one the members of the herd followed each other into the rushing, dangerous river. Soon there was a mad crush of centrosaurs leaping headlong from the banks into the water. Some found a footing or were able to control their swim. Others, particularly the old and young, were not so strong and were rapidly lost to the merciless river. The rush of the crossing accelerated into a frenzy as the animals at the rear of the crowd pushed ahead to follow their kind.

Several hundred members of the herd were lost that day to the raging river. Their bodies floated downstream. Some got stuck on the riverbanks, others collided with logs and became like dams, temporarily blocking the flow of the river.

At a sharp curve in the river about a quarter mile downstream from the crossing, many hundreds of bodies got stuck on the banks, unable to make the turn with the current. There they would lie as days and weeks passed, diverting the water as the river returned to normal. Pools of tepid water surrounded the carcasses as they rotted in the sun. Small predatory dinosaurs came calling, picking over the bodies for as long as they were able— until the flesh became too dry to eat. As the bodies were reduced to broken skeletons, the river gradually buried the remains of the centrosaurs in thick blankets of muddy sand.

Far away, on the other side of the river, the surviving members of the centrosaur group were taking care of their newly hatched young. One day soon they too would return to cross the dangerous river and continue the cycle of life of the horned dinosaurs.

Author's Note—The preceding dinosaur story is fiction but is based on scientific evidence and ideas suggested by paleontologists. You will find explanations to support these ideas in the chapters that follow. Use the following guide to find some of these references:

- Growth of horns and frills: page 51 (Beaks, Horns, and Fancy Frills)

- Use of horns and frills: page 59 (Why Horns and Frills?)

- Herding and migration: page 89 (Safety in Numbers)

- Posture and locomotion: page 41 (Anatomy)

CHAPTER 1

DINOSAURS DEFINED

What are dinosaurs? They were reptiles, but they were a special kind that no longer exists today. Many people assume that all dinosaurs were gigantic. Some confuse the dinosaurs with extinct reptiles that flew (the pterosaurs) and those reptiles that lived in the sea (e.g., plesiosaurs, ichthyosaurs, and mosasaurs). How does one know for sure whether a creature was a dinosaur or not?

Dinosaurs came in many shapes and sizes. Some were many times larger than the largest land animals alive today. Others were as small as chickens. There were carnivores (they ate meat) and herbivores (they ate plants). Some dinosaurs walked on two legs, others on four legs. Yet, in spite of these vast differences, vertebrate paleontologists who study dinosaurs have identified many specific characteristics that allow them to classify dinosaurs as a group of related creatures, different from all others.

Dinosaurs lived only during the Mesozoic Era. The age of dinosaurs spanned from about 225 million years ago in the Late Triassic Period to the end of the Late Cretaceous Period, some 65 million years ago. Fossils dating from before or after that time are not dinosaurs. This rule also means that all dinosaurs are *extinct.* Today's birds, however, are believed to be modern relatives of the dinosaurs.

Dinosaurs were a special kind of reptile. Dinosaurs had basic characteristics common to all reptiles. They had a backbone and scaly skin, and they laid eggs. Meat-eating dinosaurs were also the ancestors of birds, with some showing birdlike features such as clawed feet, hollow bones, and even feathers.

Dinosaurs were land animals. Reptiles that flew in the air or lived in the water were around at the same time as dinosaurs, but they were *not* dinosaurs. Dinosaurs were built to walk and live on land only, although they may have occasionally waded in the water.

Dinosaurs had special skeletal features. Dinosaurs walked differently than other reptiles because of their hips. Dinosaurs had either ornithischian ("birdlike") hips or saurischian ("lizardlike") hips. Both kinds of hips allowed dinosaurs to walk with their legs tucked under their bodies to support their full weight. This mammal- or birdlike stance is clearly different from the sprawling stance of today's reptiles. A dinosaur would never have dragged its stomach along the ground like a crocodile or lizard. Other distinguishing skeletal features of dinosaurs include:

- Three or more vertebrae (back bones) attaching the spine to the hip.

- A ball-and-socket joint attaching the legs to the hip for increased mobility and flexibility.

- High ankles and long foot bones. (Dinosaurs walked on their toes.)

- A simple hinge joint at the ankle.

- Three or fewer finger bones on the fourth finger of each forefoot (hand), or no fourth finger at all.

- Three to five clawed or hoofed toes on the hind foot.

Understanding Dinosaurs

The study of extinct fossil organisms is called paleontology. (*Paleo* means "ancient.") Paleontologists use fossil traces of ancient organisms as a window onto life in the distant past, before the evolution of modern man.

Most of what we know about dinosaurs comes from our knowledge of their fossilized skeletons and the layers of earth in which they are found. Putting a dinosaur together is like doing a jigsaw puzzle without a picture to follow. Fortunately, because dinosaurs were vertebrates, all dinosaur skeletons are similar in some ways. A basic knowledge of vertebrate skeletons, and of dinosaur skeletons in particular, helps guide the paleontologist when putting together a new fossil jigsaw puzzle.

While no human being has ever seen a dinosaur in the flesh, much can be revealed by studying the fossil clues. The paleontologist must have a firm grasp of scientific methods

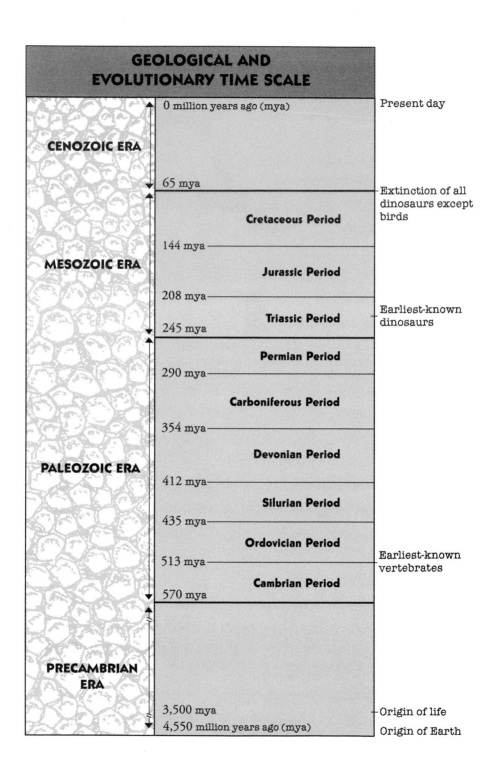

GEOLOGICAL AND EVOLUTIONARY TIME SCALE

CENOZOIC ERA	0 million years ago (mya)	Present day
	65 mya	Extinction of all dinosaurs except birds
MESOZOIC ERA	Cretaceous Period	
	144 mya	
	Jurassic Period	
	208 mya	
	Triassic Period	Earliest-known dinosaurs
	245 mya	
PALEOZOIC ERA	Permian Period	
	290 mya	
	Carboniferous Period	
	354 mya	
	Devonian Period	
	412 mya	
	Silurian Period	
	435 mya	
	Ordovician Period	Earliest-known vertebrates
	513 mya	
	Cambrian Period	
	570 mya	
PRECAMBRIAN ERA	3,500 mya	Origin of life
	4,550 million years ago (mya)	Origin of Earth

and fact. He or she must also have a good imagination and a knack for solving mysteries. Fossils provide evidence for the construction of dinosaurs. The paleontologist examines these facts and tries to understand how they affected dinosaur lifestyle and behavior.

Our knowledge of dinosaurs grows every year. This book, and others in the series, will help you understand the many kinds of dinosaurs and how they lived. It is based on the latest scientific evidence and shows us that dinosaur science is alive and well all over the world. After all, if scientific estimates are correct, there may have been as many as 1,200 unique kinds, or genera, of dinosaurs, only about 350 of which have yet been discovered.[1] If you decide to make a career out of dinosaur science, maybe one day you will add a new dinosaur or two to the list.

The Ceratopsians

When it comes to the dinosaurs, the ceratopsians were latecomers. Their first traces go back only about 150 million years to the latter part of the Early Cretaceous Period. By the time they walked the earth, more than two thirds of the known dinosaurs had already become extinct.

The name *ceratopsian* means "horned-face," after the most famous members of the group such as *Triceratops* ("three-horned face"). These magnificent beasts were adorned with impressive horns on the nose and brow. They also had a large bony neck frill encircling the rear of their head. These frills often sported several sharp spikes or bony knobs, like a warrior's shield. The largest horned dinosaurs, such as *Triceratops*, were huge, tank-sized creatures. It has long been a pastime of dinosaur lovers to imagine a pitched battle between the plant-eater *Triceratops* and the largest predator of the time, *Tyrannosaurus rex*, or *T. rex* ("tyrant lizard"). With its nearly impenetrable head armor and long pointed horns, one can probably assume that a healthy adult *Triceratops* could injure or kill many an attacking *T. rex*.

Triceratops

There were three families of ceratopsians: psittacosaurs, protoceratopsids, and ceratopsids. They were not all huge. Some did not even have horns. The psittacosaurs, found in eastern Asia, were only as large as a medium-sized dog. Protoceratopsids, found in Asia and North America, were about the size of a large dog. These creatures had bony beaks and only a hint of the horny adornments found on their larger cousins, the ceratopsids.

Along with the iguanodonts and duck-billed dinosaurs, the horned dinosaurs were highly developed plant-eating machines. They probably snipped and chewed their way through plants and shrubs on the ground like gigantic hedge trimmers. The design of their jaws, teeth, and the muscles that powered them is one of the great success stories in the evolution of plant-eating dinosaurs.

Even though their time was short by dinosaur standards, the ceratopsians are one of the better known kinds of

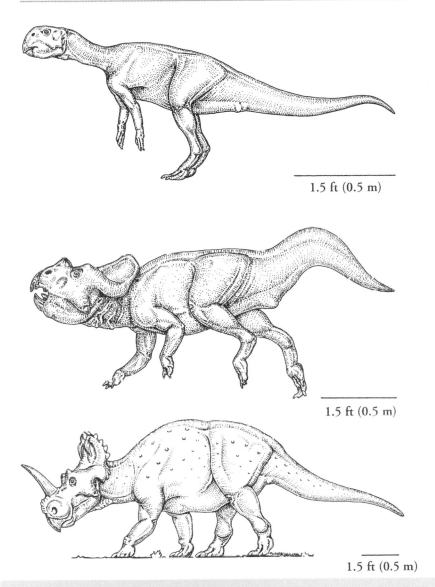

1.5 ft (0.5 m)

1.5 ft (0.5 m)

1.5 ft (0.5 m)

Ceratopsians existed in three distinct forms during the Early to Late Cretaceous Periods. Typical examples are the following: *Psittacosaurus* (top) was a small bipedal ceratopsian without horns. *Protoceratops* (middle) was a small to medium sized dinosaur with a frill but no horns. *Centrosaurus* (bottom) was one of the largest of the ceratopsians and had a long, sharp horn.

dinosaurs. There is evidence that these great animals traveled in large herds and nested in common areas with others of their kind. Some ceratopsians—such as *Triceratops, Protoceratops* ("first horned face"), and *Centrosaurus* ("horned lizard")—are represented by dozens or even hundreds of fossil skeletons, a remarkable stroke of luck for paleontologists. Unfortunately, some of the lesser known members of the ceratopsians are known from skimpy evidence, leaving many mysteries and gaps in the understanding of the origin and evolution of these unique creatures. Another curious fact about ceratopsians is that they have been found only in the Northern Hemisphere, and no ceratopsian with actual horns has ever been found outside of North America.

The ceratopsians existed in great numbers, but there were relatively few kinds compared to some other varieties of dinosaurs. Only about 7 percent of all the individual kinds, or genera, of dinosaurs recognized so far are ceratopsians. Even so, three of the horned dinosaurs—*Protoceratops, Psittacosaurus* ("parrot lizard"), and *Triceratops*—are among the best known of all dinosaurs based on an abundance of fossil specimens. Although we may be able to name a larger number of different kinds of meat-eating dinosaurs, the ceratopsians and other plant-eaters on which they fed greatly outnumbered them.

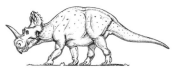

Protoceratops

The first recognizable horned dinosaur discovered was the incredible *Triceratops*, a ceratopsid. Although a pair of its

144 mya (million years ago)   65 mya

Early Cretaceous	Late Cretaceous

Psittacosaurs

Protoceratopsids

Ceratopsids

Three distinct groups of ceratopsians evolved during the age of dinosaurs.

horns had been previously discovered, nobody recognized this creature for what it was until a complete skull was unearthed in 1889. It was the last major group of dinosaurs ever discovered. It was a major surprise for paleontologists, and proved once again that just when we thought we understood the dinosaurs, they offered us another magnificent treat. The discovery of weird and wonderful horned dinosaurs continues to this day. These were some of the most unusual beasts ever to walk the earth.

CHAPTER 2

ORIGINS AND EVOLUTION

When the first dinosaurs evolved, they were part of a rich biological history that had already spanned hundreds of millions of years.

Dinosaurs descended from land vertebrates. Land vertebrates descended from ocean vertebrates, which began wandering onto land about 370 million years ago. All of these early animals lived at least part of their lives in the water. Even today's amphibians, which take to the land as adults, begin as waterborne creatures. Adult amphibians still need to return to the water to lay their eggs.

The most important biological event leading to true land animals was the evolution of the amniotes, vertebrate animals that could fertilize their eggs internally. These included reptiles and birds, which lay shelled eggs on land, and mammals, whose fertilized eggs develop within their bodies. Humans,

Vertebrate Origins and Evolution
Leading to Dinosaurs

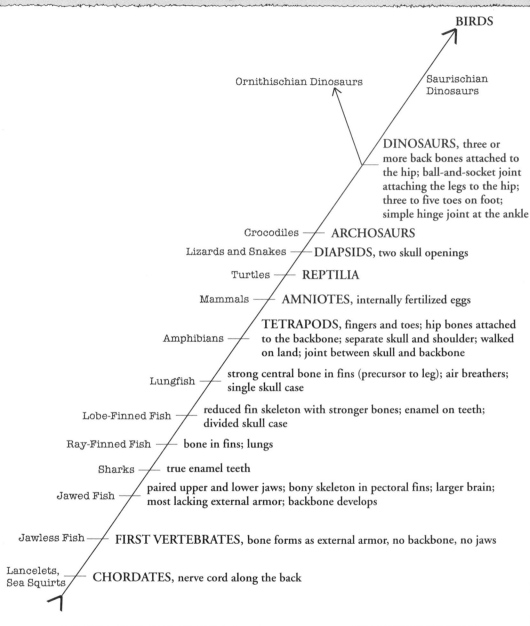

BIRDS

Ornithischian Dinosaurs

Saurischian
Dinosaurs

DINOSAURS, three or
more back bones attached to
the hip; ball-and-socket joint
attaching the legs to the hip;
three to five toes on foot;
simple hinge joint at the ankle

Crocodiles — ARCHOSAURS

Lizards and Snakes — DIAPSIDS, two skull openings

Turtles — REPTILIA

Mammals — AMNIOTES, internally fertilized eggs

TETRAPODS, fingers and toes; hip bones attached
Amphibians — to the backbone; separate skull and shoulder; walked
on land; joint between skull and backbone

strong central bone in fins (precursor to leg); air breathers;
Lungfish — single skull case

Lobe-Finned Fish — reduced fin skeleton with stronger bones; enamel on teeth;
divided skull case

Ray-Finned Fish — bone in fins; lungs

Sharks — true enamel teeth

paired upper and lower jaws; bony skeleton in pectoral fins; larger brain;
Jawed Fish — most lacking external armor; backbone develops

Jawless Fish — FIRST VERTEBRATES, bone forms as external armor, no backbone, no jaws

Lancelets,
Sea Squirts — CHORDATES, nerve cord along the back

Figure 1. This diagram shows how vertebrate animals evolved to yield dinosaurs.
The steps along the way include evolutionary changes that are directly
related to the traits of dinosaurs. The time span from the appearance of the
first chordates to the last dinosaur is about 460 million years.

birds, lizards, snakes, turtles, and even dinosaurs are all related by being amniotes.

Dinosaurs fall within the class of vertebrates known as Reptilia, or reptiles. Reptiles are egg-laying backboned animals with scaly skin. The different kinds of reptiles, living and extinct, are categorized by certain features of their skeletons. Most important is the design of the reptilian skull. Dinosaurs fall within the subclass Diapsida, which includes reptiles whose skulls had a pair of openings behind each eye. Diapsida is divided into two groups. The lepidosaurs consist of the kinds of lizards and snakes that live today. The archosaurs consist of thecodonts (a group of reptiles from the Triassic Period), crocodiles (living and extinct), pterosaurs (extinct flying reptiles), and dinosaurs (extinct except for birds).[1] All dinosaurs are probably descendants of a single common archosaur ancestor.[2]

The dinosaurs and other reptiles of the Diapsida were some of the most successful land vertebrates of all time. Dinosaurs first appeared about 225 million years ago and began to spread rapidly by the end of the Triassic Period.[3] Figure 1 summarizes the evolution of vertebrates leading to the dinosaurs and their bird descendents.

Dinosaur Beginnings

The archosaurs included a variety of reptiles of many sizes, some of which led to the dinosaurs. Some evolved as four-legged creatures with sprawling legs, while others gradually began to walk or sprint for short distances on their two hind legs. By the Late Triassic Period, about 225 million years ago, some two-legged, meat-eating archosaurs had evolved specialized hips and legs to help them stand erect. This supported the full weight of their bodies while walking on two feet. They ranged in size from about 6 inches (15 centimeters) to 13 feet (4 meters). These kinds of archosaurs led to the first dinosaurs.

By the early part of the Late Triassic Period, two distinct branches of dinosaurs had evolved based on their hip designs. The saurischians (lizard-hipped dinosaurs) included the meat-eating theropods and plant-eating sauropods. The ornithischians (bird-hipped dinosaurs) included the remaining assortment of plant eaters such as ornithopods (duckbills, iguanodonts, and others) and armored and horned dinosaurs.

The earliest horned dinosaurs first appeared in the Early Cretaceous Period, about 150 million years ago. This was relatively late in the evolution of dinosaurs. Their remains have been found only in the eastern Asian locations of Mongolia, China, and southern Siberia. By the time they appeared, Asia was already rich with a wide variety of meat- and plant-eating dinosaurs. The long-necked sauropods were the dominant herbivores. Many other kinds of low-browsing herbivorous dinosaurs walked alongside them, including the early ornithopods, armored dinosaurs, and plated stegosaurs. Giant predatory dinosaurs were also present at that time, as were the early dromaeosaurs, or "raptors," small and fierce meat eaters equipped with killing claws on their feet.

The ceratopsians were good at chewing some of the toughest low-growing plants. Other herbivores may have found these woody plants more difficult to eat. This gave the ceratopsians a special place in the world of plant-eating dinosaurs.

The Ceratopsian Groups

All horned dinosaurs are included in the order Ceratopsia. The name *Ceratopsia* means "horned face." You may wonder why this name is given to the group even though some members do not have horns. The name was created during the nineteenth century, when the only ceratopsians known were the large varieties with distinctive horns and neck frills. The smaller, hornless varieties—such as *Psittacosaurus* and *Protoceratops*—are clearly related to the horned varieties but were discovered after the name *ceratopsians* had been established. The families of Psittacosauridae and Protoceratopsidae were created to include the hornless kinds of ceratopsians.

Ceratopsia is divided into two main groups, the Psittacosauria and the Neoceratopsia. The Psittacosauridae includes only the psittacosaurs, a separate branch of the horned dinosaurs. The Neoceratopsia includes the two families of the most familiar horned dinosaurs, the Protoceratopsidae and the Ceratopsidae.

In 1999, a primitive horned dinosaur named *Chaoyangsaurus* ("Chaoyang lizard") was discovered in China. It dates from the beginning of the Early Cretaceous Period. It has some of the characteristics of both the protoceratopsids and ceratopsids, which came later, and appears to be a common ancestor to them both. Once it was thought that the psittacosaurs were the ancestors of the other horned dinosaurs.[4] The presence of *Chaoyangsaurus* instead suggests that the psittacosaurs were a side branch of the Ceratopsia family tree, rather than the direct ancestors of the protoceratopsids and ceratopsids. Going back even further in time, it is likely that the deeper roots of all Ceratopsia are with the ornithopods, but specimens to prove this have not yet been discovered.[5]

Ceratopsians had ornithischian (birdlike) hips, one of the two kinds of hips seen in dinosaurs. They were all herbivores. An early family of Ceratopsia was the psittacosaurs. They were only about 6.5 feet (2 meters) long, including the tail, and weighed about as much as a German shepherd. They were primarily bipedal, walking on their long back legs. Most notable was their parrotlike beak, after which they were named. This was the forerunner of the beak seen in all ceratopsians. Like the later horned dinosaurs, psittacosaurs had cheek teeth designed

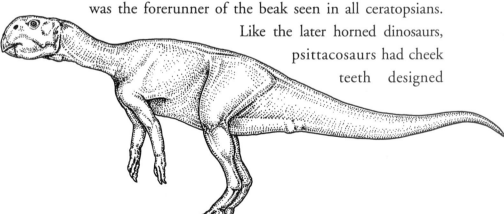

The psittacosaurs, such as *Psittacosaurus*, were primarily bipedal. They walked on their long back legs.

Psittacosauridae ("parrot lizard")

Early and primitive ceratopsians about as big as a medium-sized dog. They were notable for their parrotlike beak, cutting teeth situated in the cheek area, long legs, three functional fingers, and four weight-bearing toes. Found only in eastern Asia.

Time: Early Cretaceous Period

Psittacosaurus

Protoceratopsidae ("first horned face")

Early and small ceratopsians about as big as a large-sized dog. They had an oversized head with large, strong jaws, shearing teeth situated in the cheek area, and a sharp beak. They also had a bony neck frill and a ridge along the nose that grew larger with age. Found in eastern Asia and western North America.

Time: Early to Late Cretaceous Period

Bagaceratops,
Graciliceratops,
Leptoceratops,
Montanoceratops,
Archaeoceratops,
Zuniceratops

Protoceratops

Ceratopsidae ("horned face")

The largest ceratopsians, which often exceeded a rhinoceros in size. They had the cutting cheek teeth and bony beaks of their ancestors but also had one, two, or three face horns on the nose and brow, and large ornamental bony frills. They are divided into two groups; the Centrosaurinae with short frills and the Chasmosaurinae with long frills. Found only in western North America.

Triceratops, Torosaurus,
Pentaceratops,
Styracosaurus,
Einiosaurus

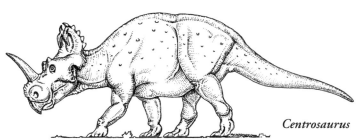

Centrosaurus

Time: Late Cretaceous Period

Some ceratopsians are still not understood well enough to place them in these families. One of these is *Chaoyangsaurus* from the Late Jurassic Period, which may have been the common ancestor of both protoceratopsids and ceratopsids.

for cutting tough vegetation. They also had a bony ridge around the back of the head that hinted at the large neck frill seen in other ceratopsians.

The next oldest variety of ceratopsians were the protoceratopsids. They were also small dinosaurs. Although they walked primarily on four legs, they could probably rear up or even run on their hind legs when needed.

The largest of the horned dinosaurs were the ceratopsids. With some larger than today's rhinoceroses, they thundered along on four legs and were decorated with exquisite horns and frills.

Many of the ceratopsians are well known from abundant fossil specimens. Most dinosaurs are known from only about five specimens per kind, or genus. With horned dinosaurs, there are about nine or ten specimens per genus and sometimes many more.[6] Because these creatures lived during the most recent part of the age of dinosaurs, the likelihood is greater that scientists will find their fossils. This is because their bones have had less time to sit in the earth and weather away than some of the earlier dinosaurs.

The ceratopsians can be divided into distinct families based on common characteristics. The chart on page 33 is a summary of ceratopsian families. It is organized chronologically by family and includes the names of members that are best known from the fossil evidence.

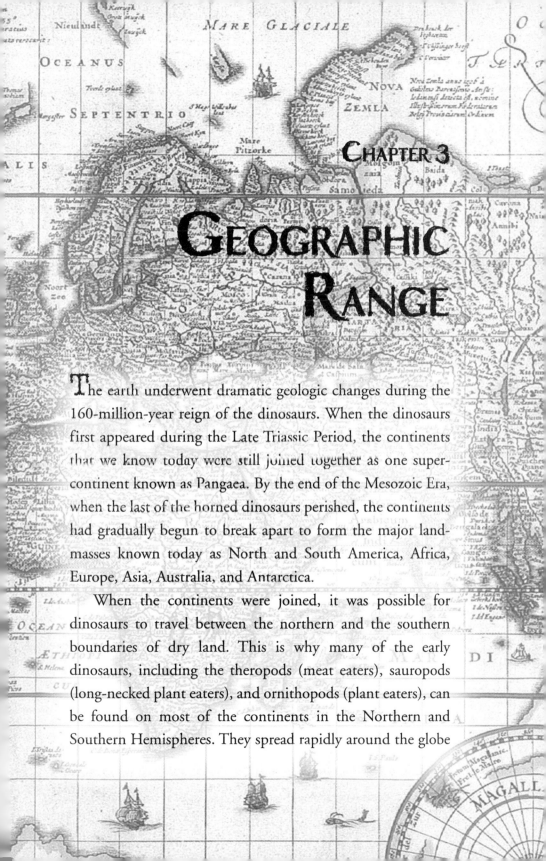

Chapter 3

Geographic Range

The earth underwent dramatic geologic changes during the 160-million-year reign of the dinosaurs. When the dinosaurs first appeared during the Late Triassic Period, the continents that we know today were still joined together as one supercontinent known as Pangaea. By the end of the Mesozoic Era, when the last of the horned dinosaurs perished, the continents had gradually begun to break apart to form the major landmasses known today as North and South America, Africa, Europe, Asia, Australia, and Antarctica.

When the continents were joined, it was possible for dinosaurs to travel between the northern and the southern boundaries of dry land. This is why many of the early dinosaurs, including the theropods (meat eaters), sauropods (long-necked plant eaters), and ornithopods (plant eaters), can be found on most of the continents in the Northern and Southern Hemispheres. They spread rapidly around the globe

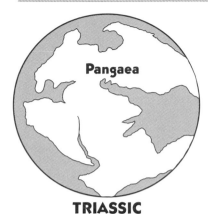

TRIASSIC

EARLY JURASSIC

EARLY CRETACEOUS

while the continents were still connected. By the time of the horned dinosaurs, however, in the middle and later parts of the Cretaceous Period, the Northern and Southern Hemispheres had split apart. This made migration from the Northern Hemisphere to the Southern Hemisphere impossible. Horned dinosaurs appear to have originated in the Northern Hemisphere, probably in Asia. They are found only in North America and Asia. North America was connected to Europe and Asia by a land bridge during the earlier part of the Late Cretaceous Period. This accounts for similarities between early horned dinosaurs—the protoceratopsids—found in eastern Asia and western North America. Today's arrangement of the continents was substantially formed during the end of the Cretaceous Period, the end of the dinosaur era.

The map on the next pages illustrates the range of ceratopsian fossil locations. Fossils from these dinosaurs have been found in North America and Asia.

Range of
Fossil
Around

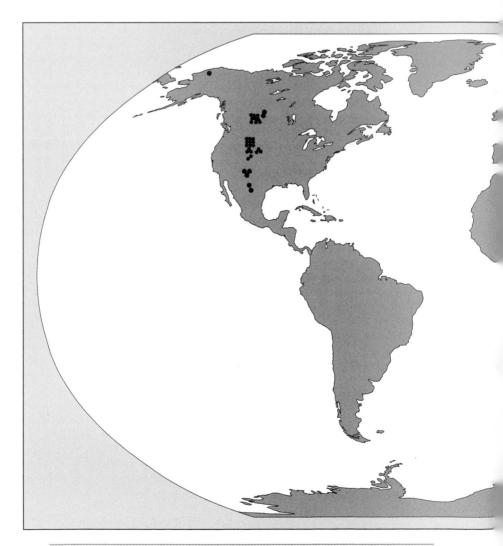

Ceratopsian Locations the World

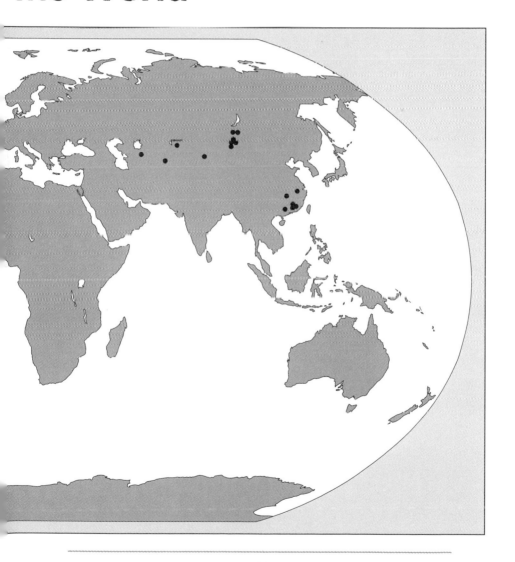

ANATOMY

All organisms are made up of biological systems, such as the skeletal and muscular systems. The study of these structures is called anatomy. Studying the anatomy of an organism is different from studying how the structures are *used* in the organism. This type of study, physiology, is covered in the next chapter.

Dinosaurs Are Vertebrates

Dinosaurs are part of the lineage of animals known as vertebrates—animals with backbones. The first vertebrates were fish, followed by amphibians, reptiles, dinosaurs, and mammals and birds. To the best of our knowledge, the first vertebrates appeared about 500 million years ago in the form of jawless fish.[1] Dinosaurs first walked the earth about 225 million years ago, nearly 275 million years after fish had begun to populate the oceans.

Regardless of whether they live in the water, walk on the land, or fly in the air, all vertebrates share some common characteristics. The most basic common feature of the vertebrate body is that one side of the body is a mirror image of the other. This trait is called bilateral symmetry.

A second common feature is that the organs of vertebrates have descended from what were basically the same organs in their ancestors. This idea is called the principle of homology.

Dinosaurs shared many similar skeletal features with other vertebrates, living and extinct. Even though we rarely, if ever, see the actual remains of soft tissue or organs of the dinosaurs—such as the brain, lungs, liver, and gut—we can assume that they shared most of the internal organs of today's land-dwelling vertebrates. These features allow scientists to piece together what living dinosaurs must have been like.

The Dinosaur Hip

All dinosaurs are divided into two large groups based on the structure of their hip bones. The saurischian ("lizard-hipped") group is comprised of the two-legged carnivorous theropods; the four-legged, long-necked herbivorous sauropods; and their sister group, the two-legged herbivorous prosauropods. The ornithischian ("bird-hipped") group includes all others such as plated, armored, horned, duck-billed, and iguanodontid dinosaurs. All ceratopsians were ornithischians.

Both kinds of dinosaur hips allowed the hind legs to be attached underneath the body so that they could bear the entire weight of the creature. The hind legs were also connected to the hip with a ball-and-socket joint. This provided dinosaurs with increased flexibility and mobility over their reptile ancestors. The front legs were positioned underneath

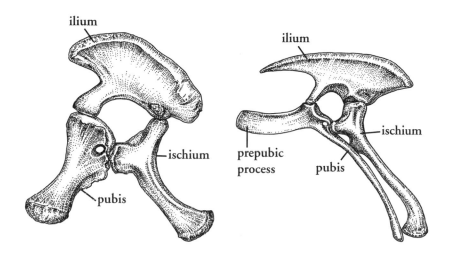

There are two kinds of dinosaur hips: saurischian ("lizard-hipped," left) and ornithiscian ("bird-hipped," right).

the body to help bear the weight of those dinosaurs that walked on all fours.

The legs of a modern reptile, such as a crocodile or lizard, are attached to the sides of their body and do not support the full weight of their body while the creature is at rest. Reptiles lay their bellies on the ground and rise up only when they need to move. On the other hand, the position of a dinosaur was "always up." Dinosaurs must have been more active and energetic than today's reptiles simply because it required more stamina to hold up their body weight.

Dinosaur legs were designed more like those of mammals or birds but with some clear distinctions. While the joints in their shoulders and hips were highly flexible, those in the knees and elbows were not. This, combined with an ankle that was more like a door hinge than a ball and socket, restricted the bending of a dinosaur's forelimbs and hind limbs to one plane of motion, forward or backward. Unlike humans and other mammals, which can move sideways with ease, a dinosaur had to turn its body to face the direction it wanted to go to move to the side. Dinosaurs would have made lousy soccer goalies.

The Ceratopsian Body

Ceratopsians ranged in size from the puny 6.5-foot- (2-meter) long psittacosaurs to the larger-than-elephant-sized 30-foot- (9-meter-) long horned dinosaurs. For 75 million years, they evolved into larger and larger creatures until their demise 65 million years ago. During this time, they became one of the dominant plant-eating dinosaurs, thanks to the development of sturdy jaws and sets of plant-chopping teeth. Together with the duck-billed dinosaurs, they occupied the plant-eating role that had once been filled by the gigantic sauropods.

The three families of ceratopsians—the psittacosaurs, protoceratopsids, and ceratopsids—vary in size and appearance. But a close examination of their bodies, and the skulls in particular, reveal the features that unite them with a common ancestor.

All ceratopsians shared the following features:

- They had ornithischian hips.

- Their heads were large for the size of their bodies.

- They had a narrow, toothless, bony beak. It was made of two parts. The bottom was attached to the front of the lower jaw. The top was attached to the front of the upper jaw and extended high between the nasal openings. In life, this beak was covered with a sheath, like that of a modern bird.

- Their skulls were triangular (when viewed from the top down; see page 54), with the beak at the front and narrowest point.

- Their skulls flared wide at the cheeks. The teeth were located within this area. The wide cheek probably served as a pouch during eating.

- They had five digits on each forelimb and four on each hind limb.

- There was a broad overhang at the back of the skull, represented by a frill in most ceratopsians. In the psittacosaurs, there is only a ridge. The frill was an outgrowth of the top and side bones of the rear of the skull.

In addition to the common characteristics among all ceratopsians, the following features further distinguish each of the three groups from one another.

Psittacosaur Anatomy

- Psittacosaurs were small, no longer than 6.5 feet (2 meters).

- The outline of the snout and beak were parrotlike when viewed from the side.

- The distance from the eye to the front of the skull was proportionately shorter than in any other kind of dinosaur.[2]

- They had six fused (joined) back bones over the hip (sacral vertebrae).

- They had three functional fingers that could probably bear weight if the animal wanted to lean down or walk slowly on all fours. The other two fingers on each hand were greatly reduced in size when compared to other ceratopsians.

- *Psittacosaurus* had short, stubby claws on its hands and feet.

- It probably walked on two legs most of the time but could walk on all fours if needed.

- The neck frill was small and appeared as only a short ridge around the back of the skull.

- The teeth were designed for grinding tough plant material.

Protoceratopsid Anatomy

- Protoceratopsids were small, the largest being about 10 feet (3 meters) long.

- The neck frill was pronounced but small. It was solid in some of the earliest species but had openings in its bony framework in later members of the group.

- They walked primarily on four legs, although they could probably move about on two legs if necessary.

- They had six to eight fused (joined) back bones over the hip (sacral vertebrae).

- Protoceratopsids had short, stubby claws on their hands and feet.

- Their teeth were designed for grinding tough plant material.

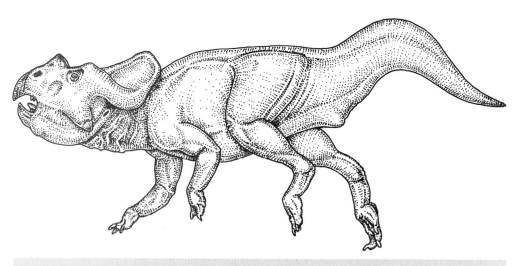

Protoceratops walked primarily on four legs.

Ceratopsid Anatomy

- Ceratopsids were large and heavy, the largest being about 26 feet (8 meters) long.

- They had from one to three horns on the nose and brow. One group, the pachyrhinosaurs, had a wide, flattened nasal bump or "boss" instead of horns. Horns were most likely used for protection as well as for combat between rival males.

- The neck frill was well developed and often large. It was made of solid bone in some members, such as *Triceratops*, but had openings in its bony framework in most others. The openings looked like round windows in the bony outline of the frill.

Centrosaurus (with a female adult for scale) was a 17-foot-long, short-frilled ceratopsian.

- Because their heads were so large and heavy, especially with the weight of the bony frill, the first four bones of the neck were fused (joined) together to give it strength.

- They were primarily four-legged walkers. Their hind limbs were firmly positioned in an erect posture underneath their bodies, but their front legs bent out somewhat at the elbows. They probably could trot or gallop on occasion, but they could not run swiftly. In contrast, the modern-day rhinoceros has front legs that allow it to run faster than a ceratopsid could.

- The nasal openings were enlarged and connected to an extended network of nasal passages that may have been used to ventilate the brain directly in the large head.

- They had ten fused (joined) back bones over the hip (sacral vertebrae).

- Their toes were rounded and blunt on both the hands and feet.

- They had extensive sets of teeth. The teeth were not designed for grinding food, but for shearing it like scissors.

- Their skulls included an extra space between the outer wall and the braincase. This probably acted as a shock absorber to protect the brain during head-butting contests between rival males.

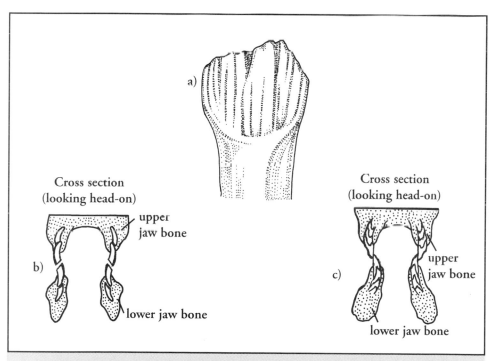

a) The primitive pattern of a *Psittacosaurus* tooth. b) A cross section of a *Protoceratops* jaw shows a single backup replacement tooth. c) This cross section of a *Triceratops* jaw illustrates how the teeth in the upper and lower jaws formed a cutting surface that sliced through vegetation. Each tooth position is backed up by a series of replacements.

Dinosaur Skin

Dinosaur skin, like other soft body parts of these animals, was almost never fossilized. The skin of dinosaurs easily decomposed and disappeared long before fossilization could take place. Although there is some evidence about dinosaur skin, it is extremely rare, especially for ceratopsians.

Dinosaur skin impressions and fossils are the only clear evidence we have for what dinosaurs may have looked like on the outside. Artists who specialize in the reproduction of dinosaurs are particularly interested in skin impressions so that they can make their drawings as accurate as possible.

All of the evidence uncovered so far regarding dinosaur skin shows that they had nonoverlapping scales similar to those of modern monitor lizards. These scales varied in size across different parts of the body. They were generally smaller, for flexibility, around the head and joints such as the neck and knees and larger along broad parts of the body and tail.

Several intriguing fossils of ceratopsian skin impressions have been discovered. The most notable is an impression found with a specimen of *Chasmosaurus* ("wide opening lizard") in 1925.[3] Such fossil impressions are *not* the dinosaur skin itself, but the pattern of the skin that was left behind in the mud where a dinosaur died. These impressions are known as trace fossils. They represent a "trace" of the dinosaur that made them rather than being the fossilized parts of the dinosaur itself. In the case of this one *Chasmosaurus* specimen, the skin impression came from the hip region. The skin was composed of rows of large circular plates about 2 inches

(51 millimeters) in diameter. The rows were divided by smaller, irregularly shaped plates.[4] Scientists have not reported evidence of the skin around the head or frill region, so what the horned dinosaur had there is pure speculation.

Skin color was never preserved in skin impressions or fossils. However, scientists can guess that the color of dinosaurs varied, as color does in today's reptiles and birds. Some dinosaurs, especially the smaller ones, may have had camouflaging colors to help them blend in with their surroundings. Color may have also been a way to tell the difference between males and females of the species and as a means for attracting a mate.

Beaks, Horns, and Fancy Frills—Ceratopsian Skulls

For anyone who likes to study the skulls of animals, extinct or otherwise, the horned dinosaurs are a dream. They had some of the most remarkable, unlikely, and positively unusual head-gear to adorn any of nature's creatures. Even in the realm of dinosaur skulls, where unusual shapes are common, horned dinosaur skulls are second to none.

The three different kinds of ceratopsians differed widely in the overall size and design of their skulls and jaws. The skulls ranged in size from a petite 6 inches (15 centimeters) for *Psittacosaurus* to a record-breaking 6.5 to 9 feet (2.0 to 2.7 meters) for *Torosaurus* ("piercing lizard") and *Pentaceratops* ("five-horned face"). These are the largest skulls of any known land animals.[5]

Psittacosaur Skulls

The small skulls of the psittacosaurs were square when viewed from the side. The skull bones were mostly thin and delicate and had large openings for the eye and behind the eye. The strongest parts of the skull, and the only aspect of this dinosaur that might be considered horns, were thickened bony points jutting out from the cheeks. The beak was shaped very much like that of a parrot.

Psittacosaur teeth were in the cheek area, like other ceratopsians, but the similarities end there. This early ceratopsian had widely spaced teeth with both rounded and ridged crowns. These were somewhat like those of early ornithopods, which is one reason paleontologists believe that both groups of dinosaurs originated from a common ancestor that has not been discovered yet. The teeth were designed for cutting and grinding vegetation. In contrast, the horned giants such as *Triceratops* developed complex sets of teeth for shredding tough plant material but not grinding it.

Protoceratopsid Skulls

The skull of *Protoceratops* and its close relatives were also at the small end of the ceratopsian scale, at about 22 inches (55 centimeters) long. They were the first ceratopsians to have a distinctive frill along the rear of the skull. This frill covered and protected the animal's vulnerable neck and probably served as a means to display differences between males and females.

So many specimens of *Protoceratops* have been discovered that the entire growth cycle of this dinosaur can be studied from hatchling to adult. The frill developed early in the life of these dinosaurs. It had two large holes in it that were presumably covered by skin. By the time *Protoceratops* was half adult size, the frill took on either a high and wide shape or a low and narrow shape. The difference in shape may have indicated which were males and which were females (see Chapter 5). Some protoceratopsians, including *Leptoceratops* ("slender-horned face"), have been discovered in North America. Their frills were smaller than their Asian relatives.

In addition to the frill, as *Protoceratops* got older it developed a bony ridge along the center of its skull, like an arch in front of the eyes. This may have been used in butting contests between competing males.

The beak of *Protoceratops* was strong and sharp for snipping vegetation. Its teeth were well inside the mouth, lining the interior of the cheek. Its large head may have been necessary for accommodating its large jaws and jaw muscles, used to chomp the woody vegetation on which they fed. The tops, or crowns, of the teeth were leaf-shaped with ridges for snatching and grinding plants. Dinosaurs, like reptiles, always had a new tooth to replace a tooth that was lost. Since *Protoceratops* only had a single replacement tooth resting beneath each exposed tooth, it seems that this dinosaur did not lose its teeth very often.

Lateral (side) view   Dorsal (top) view

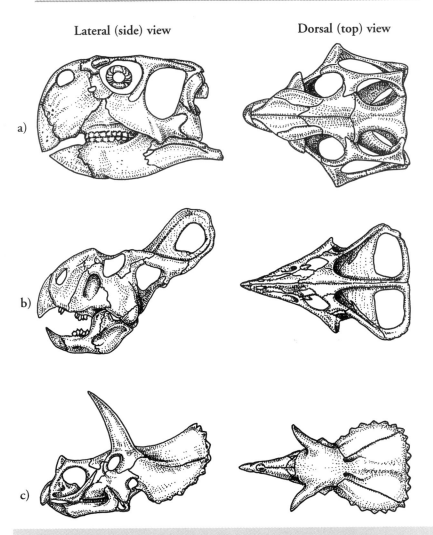

a) *Psittacosaurus* had a triangular skull that was characteristic of the ceratopsians. It had a toothless, parrotlike beak for nipping plants. The strongest part of the skull was thickened with bony points jutting out from the cheeks. b) *Protoceratops* did not have true horns. Adults developed a thick bony ridge down the centerline of the skull. c) *Triceratops* was one of the long-frilled horned dinosaurs. The large bony frill was an extension of the top and side bones of the rear of the skull.

Ceratopsid Skulls

Ceratopsids are the creatures most of us picture when we hear the term *horned dinosaurs*. Some were even big enough to stand toe-to-toe with *Tyrannosaurus*. They were the vegetarians with attitude.

Paleontologists have been obsessed by the heads of these dinosaurs ever since the naming of *Triceratops* in 1889, the first specimen of a horned dinosaur that included a good example of a skull. You might think from their names that nothing but their skulls has ever been discovered: *Triceratops* ("three-horned face"), *Pentaceratops* ("five-horned face"), *Styracosaurus* ("spiked lizard"), *Torosaurus* ("piercing lizard"), and *Pachyrhinosaurus* ("thick-nosed lizard"). The truth be told, many skeletons have been found attached to these skulls. But the skeletons are all quite similar. The fun lies in analyzing the skulls.

Because the frill is actually a part of the skull itself, two of the ceratopsids—*Torosaurus* and *Pentaceratops*—have found a place in the record books for having the longest skulls of any land creatures ever: 9 feet (2.7 meters) or longer.

Ceratopsid dinosaurs are divided into two groups based on the length of the frill and size of the nose and brow horns. The centrosaurines, or short-frilled ceratopsids, had long nasal horns and shorter frills than the other group, the chasmosaurines. The longest nose horn for a centrosaurine was found in *Styracosaurus* and measured about 24 inches (60 centimeters). Note that this measurement is for only the fossilized core of the horn. In the living creature, the horn would have

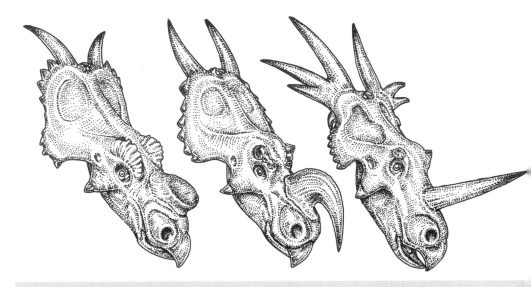

Centrosaurines, or short-frilled ceratopsians, included *Achelousaurus,* *Einiosaurus,* and *Styracosaurus.*

been covered with a bony sheath, making it several inches longer. The centrosaurines were generally smaller than the chasmosaurines. Their body lengths ranged from about 13 to 23 feet (4 to 7 meters) long and they weighed between 6,000 and 8,000 pounds (2,700 and 3,600 kilograms). They had little in the way of horns above the eyes. Their frills, however, were often elaborately adorned with spikes, bony knobs, and distinctive scalloping. Representative centrosaurines include *Centrosaurus, Monoclonius* ("single stem"), and *Styracosaurus.* The centrosaurines also include some of the most unusual headgear of all dinosaurs. Instead of a long nasal horn, *Pachyrhinosaurus* had a large blunted bump or "boss" on its nose that resembled the head of a large mallet. *Einiosaurus* ("buffalo lizard") looked like it had a giant can opener for a nasal horn.

The chasmosaurines were larger and longer than the centrosaurines, spanning a range of 17 to 30 feet (5 to 9 meters). The largest may have weighed close to 17,000 pounds (7,700 kilograms). All had long, prominent horns over the eyes and a smaller horn on the nose. *Torosaurus* had the longest of these brow horns at about 32 inches (81 centimeters). A fossil horn consists only of the bony core. In real life, it would have been covered with a fingernail-like sheath, making it longer than what is preserved as a fossil. Representative members of the chasmosaurines include *Triceratops*, *Torosaurus*, *Chasmosaurus*, and *Pentaceratops*.

Unlike their earlier relatives the psittacosaurs and protoceratopsids—whose teeth were loosely assembled and infrequently replaced—the ceratopsids developed sets of tightly packed teeth for consuming the kinds of vegetation that were common in the Late Cretaceous Period. The teeth were located in the cheek area and assembled in columns with as many as four replacement teeth below the exposed tooth at the top of each column. Counting the replacement teeth, an adult *Triceratops* had nearly 600 teeth in its mouth at any given time.[6] The columns butted up against each other to form a long cutting surface. The tops of the teeth were not flat but had a sharp ridge across the surface. When the teeth of the upper and lower jaws came together, the action was similar to a long pair of shears, slicing whatever plant material fell across

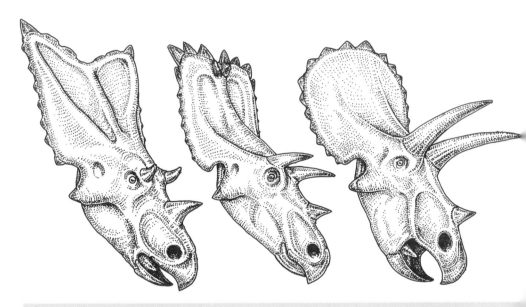

Chasmosaurines, or long-frilled ceratopsians, included *Chasmosaurus,* *Anchiceratops,* and *Triceratops.*

them. These teeth were not flat and could not be used for chewing or grinding food. The food was swallowed in large chunks, leaving the digestive tract with the task of extracting nutrients from the tough vegetation.

Why Horns and Frills?

Horns and frills make the imagination run wild about the behavior of horned dinosaurs. No one doubts that horns and frills were used for protection. One might wonder why a *Tyrannosaurus* would ever attack a full-grown bull *Triceratops*. One jab or swipe of the plant-eater's long, sharp brow horns across the predator's stomach would surely do enormous harm. The frill provided protection for the neck, normally one of the most vulnerable parts of the body. Modern African predators such as the lion and hyena will clamp down with their teeth on the neck of their victim. In doing so, they damage or even break the neck of their prey to suffocate it. One can imagine that predatory dinosaurs used a similar tactic. However, the frill of the horned dinosaurs would have been an effective shield against this kind of attack. A persistent predator, unable to bite the neck, might be faced with attacking a horned dinosaur head-on. This would have been a sure mistake in many battles.

Although paleontologists agree on the use of horns and frills for defense, the wide variety of ceratopsian skull designs has been a source of puzzlement. Why did some have brow horns and others nasal horns? Why were some horns curved up or down? What was the purpose of the elaborate scallops, knobs, and spikes that outlined the frills of many of these dinosaurs? Could horns and frills reveal more about dinosaur growth and behavior?

Frills and Jaws. One explanation for the long frills was that they were actually places where the powerful muscles of the jaws could be attached. Some paleontologists have thought that such muscles were long and stretched onto the wide flat area of the top surface of the frill.[7] This would have required a set of jaw muscles nearly 5 feet (1.5 meters) long in a dinosaur such as *Torosaurus*.[8] However, other dinosaurs with equally powerful jaws did not have such frills. The length of muscle also does not make them stronger.[9] A more reasonable theory is that the muscles were attached to the base of the frill and not farther up.[10]

Display. The frills of the horned dinosaurs varied widely between individuals of the same species. The study of the various growth stages of ceratopsians has also shown that the frill grew large and prominent when the animals reached sexual maturity. This fact alone suggests that frills, and horns as well, were not meant purely for defensive purposes, since an animal lived for most of its youth without them.[11] Instead it suggests that frills were a way to attract the attention of potential mates. Perhaps the largest and most decorative frills were viewed as belonging to the most desirable mates. Large and prominent frills may have also been colored or arrayed with various studs, spikes, and bony plates. Furthermore, when the animal was viewed face-on, the frill probably made it look much bigger. This may have been attractive to a mate but also intimidating to a predator or even another rival horned dinosaur. Lowering the head and shaking the frill from side to side might have served as a challenge or a warning to stay away.

Social Combat. The male members of several kinds of modern horned animals often use their weaponry in head-butting competition with rival males. These animals do not try to kill one another, but merely test each other to determine which is the dominant male. That is not to say that they do not cause injury in the process. It is highly likely that horned dinosaurs also behaved in this way. They may have locked nasal horns and swung their heads from side to side or butted each other to gain dominance. There is even some evidence of skull wounds due to the stabbing of one male horned dinosaur by another.[12]

The frills of the horned dinosaurs, such as *Einiosaurus*, *Styracosaurus*, and *Chasmosaurus*, helped tell one species from another.

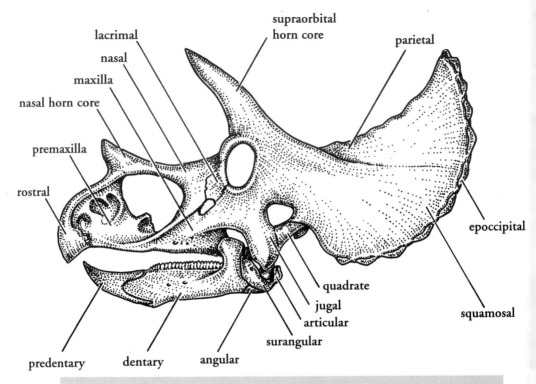

Triceratops skull, viewed from the side.

Anatomy of the *Triceratops* Skull

Skulls are composed of many small parts. Each part has its own name. Most of these parts are found in all Ceratopsia skulls, but they vary in size and shape depending on the particular kind of dinosaur. Dinosaur skulls are often found in fragments, making it important for the paleontologist to be able to recognize a certain dinosaur from the smallest of pieces. The elements found in the skull of a large ceratopsian are illustrated above using *Triceratops*.

CHAPTER 5

PHYSIOLOGY

Physiology is the study of how a body operates. The physiology of ceratopsians is understood by comparing the evidence from fossils to the anatomy and physiology of today's creatures. Other physical evidence, such as eggs and nests, has also been used to piece together what we know about the ceratopsians and other dinosaurs.

Brains and Smarts

As fascinating and large as their skulls were, the ceratopsians were sadly lacking in potential brain power. On the scale of dinosaur intelligence, they ranked near the bottom along with the notoriously dim stegosaurs, armored dinosaurs, and sauropods. To understand how this can be known, one needs to understand how the size of the brain can be used to measure an animal's "smarts."

Determining the intelligence of dinosaurs is a task that can, essentially, never be proven. After all, what *is* intelligence? Intelligence can be defined as the ability to process information or to learn. Since these are things we will never be able to observe in dinosaurs, we must rely on other clues to intelligence that are found in the fossil record. Chief among these is the size of a dinosaur's brain in comparison to the size of its body.

In examining many kinds of living animals, scientists have found a relationship between the size of the brain and the size of a creature's body. A species whose brain is larger than expected for its body size is considered more intelligent. This allows one to compare the intelligence of animals of different body sizes, say a Pekingese dog with an Irish wolfhound. By this measure, mammals and birds are considered to be more intelligent than fish, amphibians, and reptiles. What makes humans so unusual is that our brain size is seven times greater than should be expected for a creature with our body size.

The brain, like other soft tissues and organs, has not been preserved in the fossil record. However, the approximate size of a dinosaur's brain can be determined by measuring and casting the cavity in the skull where the brain once was. This cavity is called the braincase. Unfortunately, most dinosaur skull material is too incomplete to include the braincase. Even when the braincase is present, the space it enclosed is not often well preserved due to the compression and crushing of the skull during fossilization. Measurements have thus far been made for less than 5 percent of all known dinosaurs, so much work remains in this area.[1]

Scientists are fortunate to have casts of the brain cavity of at least two horned dinosaurs, *Triceratops* and *Anchiceratops* ("close horned face"). Their brain-size-to-body-size ratio was most unimpressive. Their brain power was probably somewhat comparable to that of a crocodile.[2] But what they lacked in smarts they seem to have possessed in reflexes and hulk. So, although they had the largest brain relative to body size of any four-legged herbivorous dinosaur, they were blessed with a favorable blend of instinct and body armor to make them an extremely challenging addition to any theropod's dinner.

Senses

Plant-eating creatures rely on their senses to locate food and protect themselves from danger. A good sense of smell might pick up the scent of a stalking predator or a grove of tasty vegetation over the next hill. A good sense of hearing, like smell, can provide clues to the presence of carnivores before they can be seen. Keen eyesight is important for finding food and noticing the movements of an approaching meat eater.

The senses of hearing, smell, and vision were certainly important to the ceratopsians. Evidence for these senses can be seen by studying the braincase and other parts of a dinosaur's skull.

The braincase in a dinosaur skull held the brain and the many connections between the brain and other parts of the body. Evidence of these nerve connections can be seen in the form of holes in the braincase through which nerves once attached the brain to other organs.

The brains of modern vertebrates—particularly reptiles and birds—are similar in many ways. The sense of smell is located at the front of the brain in the olfactory lobe and vision is concentrated in an optic lobe near the center.

The plant-eating *Triceratops* may have benefited from traveling in a herd, especially when faced with a stalking *Tyrannosaurus rex*.

Observing the kinds of nerve connections that exist in today's animals can help a paleontologist identify the locations of similar features in dinosaur skulls.

Braincases of at least two horned dinosaurs, *Triceratops* and *Anchiceratops*, have been found. These dinosaurs clearly had good hearing and a good sense of smell. They appear to have been well balanced and were probably surefooted, if not nimble, since a giant of these proportions can hardly be described as being light on its feet. Their eyesight was most probably good, as evidenced by the large eye sockets in their skulls. But they could look only to the sides, like a horse. Still, this kind of vision is highly effective in spotting approaching predators from either side, a key to survival. Good eyesight is also implied by the showy array of horns and frills on these creatures. These decorations most certainly existed in part to impress other horned dinosaurs.[3] It can be assumed that most other ceratopsians had senses similar to those of these two representatives of the clan.

Growth Rate

Newly hatched dinosaurs were small, yet they sometimes grew to enormous proportions that were anywhere from ten times to thousands of times their original size. What can the fossil record tell us about how fast the dinosaurs grew from hatchling to adult?

To understand how fast dinosaurs grew, scientists need to have three things. The first is a keen knowledge of how fast modern reptiles, birds, and other animals grow. Then scientists can keep their guesses about dinosaurs in perspective. Information about reptile growth is abundant. Also, reptiles continue to grow throughout their lives, unlike birds and mammals, which reach a peak size soon after reaching sexual maturity. Scientists would like to find out which of these kinds of growth applied to dinosaurs.

The second thing needed to understand the growth rates of dinosaurs is a series of fossil skeletons for a given kind of dinosaur that represents several life stages. This is available in abundance for some dinosaurs, including at least one ceratopsian, *Protoceratops*, the small-frilled plant eater from eastern Asia.

The third thing needed to understand how fast a dinosaur grew is a way in which to connect what is seen in the bones to the span of time during which a dinosaur grew. One attempt to do this uses microscopic studies of dinosaur bone. A magnified cross section of bone reveals clues about dinosaur growth. Bone tissue sometimes shows curious rings called lines of arrested growth. These growth rings are much like the seasonal rings in the cross sections of tree trunks. This phenomenon is also seen in the bones of modern reptiles. It represents an annual period when growth slows down, perhaps during a cool season when the animal is less active for an extended period. Other times, the microscopic bone pattern is smooth, without any lines. This indicates that the dinosaur was growing continuously and rapidly. No one has yet sliced up the bones of *Protoceratops* to look for microscopic evidence of growth patterns. A study of the bones of *Psittacosaurus*, however, concludes that this small dinosaur grew faster than reptiles and took about nine years to attain an adult size of about 40 pounds (18 kilograms).[4]

Another method is to compare a dinosaur's growth to that of living animals with similar biology. An ecologist named Ted Case compared the growth of *Protoceratops* to that of living reptiles. He concluded that if *Protoceratops* grew at the rate of the most rapidly growing known reptiles, it would have reached full size in twelve to twenty-three years.[5] This is not a precise answer, and we will have to wait until someone takes a closer look at the inside of ceratopsian bones to better understand their growth.

Aside from how fast the ceratopsians grew, can paleontologists tell how long an individual may have lived? This question is also tricky. A dinosaur could have lived many more years after its growth stopped. Best guesses for the life span of a dinosaur come from observing modern-day animals with similar sizes and metabolisms. One estimate of the longevity of *Psittacosaurus* suggests that it lived about ten or eleven years.[6] The larger and later horned dinosaurs probably lived longer, maybe thirty to fifty years.

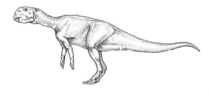

Psittacosaurus

Were Dinosaurs Warm-Blooded?

Current scientific thinking is that dinosaurs were not the slow and sluggish creatures that we once thought them to be. They were built for action and could probably move quite fast when needed. Dinosaurs also grew rapidly, outpacing the growth rate seen in many modern mammals. But not all dinosaurs were alike in this way. Some grew quite slowly, and there were many others in between.

Does this tell us whether dinosaurs were endotherms (warm-blooded) or ectotherms (cold-blooded)? This is a question that many paleontologists have argued. Unfortunately, there is no simple answer or single piece of fossil evidence that can tell us for sure.

There are two factors that determine whether an animal is warm- or cold-blooded. One is the source of heat. Was it internal, as in endotherms, or external, as in ectotherms? The other factor is the consistency of body temperature. Was it constant or variable?

If we look at today's animals, we can see that small and large mammals are warm-blooded and that reptiles of all sizes are cold-blooded. Dinosaurs were clearly evolved from reptiles, so they were originally thought to be cold-blooded. However, current thinking shows that dinosaurs were highly active and unique kinds of creatures, different than other reptiles in many ways. How could they be so active *and* be cold-blooded?

The answer lies in the huge size of many dinosaurs. There are no creatures quite like them alive today. But there is evidence that being cold-blooded does not rule out that a creature can be active and energetic and maintain a constant body temperature. Instead of obtaining most of its body heat from its own internal metabolism, as do endotherms, an ectotherm may use a method called *gigantothermy* to maintain its temperature.

Gigantothermy relies on a combination of biologic and environmental factors to work:[7]

A warm, temperate, or subtropical climate, such as that enjoyed by the dinosaurs. Heat absorbed during the day would be retained for many hours past dark in a large dinosaur.[8]

Large body size. The larger the body, the more likely that it would retain heat that was absorbed from the environment or produced internally through normal metabolic processes.

Layers of body insulation. Layers of fat and the mere volume of the gut of dinosaurs were probably capable of retaining body heat.

A digestive process producing heat. Ceratopsians digested their food using a gastric fermentation process that naturally produced heat as a by-product.

Special adaptations of the circulatory system. Blood flow and the circulatory path were used to pass heat from the core or gut of the dinosaur to its surface, where it could be safely shed to avoid overheating. The extensive surface area of the body, including the long tail, may have been part of this strategy for shedding excess heat.

All of the above reasons made it possible for the large ceratopsians and other big dinosaurs to maintain high body temperatures while still having lower cold-blooded metabolic rates. This could have made a significant difference in the survival of the ceratopsians, because a lower metabolism would have required them to eat less than if they had been warm-blooded. Lower food requirements would have allowed more dinosaurs to live than if metabolic rates and food requirements had been higher.

But the theory of gigantothermy comes with a significant problem. It does not account for the metabolic process of a small dinosaur or a large dinosaur while it was young and growing, before reaching a size during which gigantothermy could take over. This remains one of the puzzles of dinosaur metabolism. Perhaps the warm environment was enough to keep them active. This, plus the fact that they were eating more as they grew, might account for their maintaining a constant body temperature without the benefit of gigantothermy.

Ceratopsian Speed

How fast could the ceratopsians run? You may think there could be no answer. After all, no one has been able to set a dinosaur loose on a racetrack and time its laps with a stopwatch. But there are ways that paleontologists have approached this question.

Fossil footprints, or trackways, left by dinosaurs are the best evidence about the speed of dinosaurs. Scientists can use the length of the strides, the leg length of the dinosaur from the ground to the hip, and a mathematical formula to calculate the speed. A biomechanic and zoologist named Robert McNeill Alexander worked out a formula to calculate speed from trackways that is widely used today.[9] However, tracks are needed to calculate speed. Fans of the ceratopsians will be disappointed in this regard. Tracks that can be attributed to horned dinosaurs are rare.

Even though a lack of trackways inhibits scientists from calculating a precise speed, the anatomy of the ceratopsians provides solid clues to their running ability. The horned dinosaurs are sometimes depicted as galloping creatures, like rhinoceroses. In a true gallop, all four of an animal's feet are off the ground at the same time. It is doubtful that the largest of the horned dinosaurs, including *Triceratops*, *Torosaurus*, and *Pentaceratops*, could achieve such speeds. They were simply too heavy, and their front legs were bent outward from the

How fast could *Triceratops* run? Scientists believe that the fastest speed would have been a trot.

shoulder in such a way as to make it impossible for them to achieve a running gait. Horned dinosaur expert Peter Dodson concludes that the running ability of horned dinosaurs was limited to "a fast amble or possibly a trot."[10]

Males and Females

Telling males from females is not easy from skeletons. Paleontologists can be comfortable about doing this only when an abundance of skeletons from the same kind of dinosaur can be compared. They look for differences that could distinguish the males from the females. These traits are the result of sexual dimorphism—naturally occurring differences between the sexes of the same kind of animal. These come in the form of size, shape, and behavioral differences.[11]

In nature, these differences help identify the males from the females and may also have important functions. For example, male elephants have tusks that are used during combat or jousting with other males. Male deer have antlers to lock and wrestle with rivals to win the favor of a female.

In addition to being a protective shield and an anchor to which some of the jaw muscles were attached, the frill of the ceratopsians may have played an important role in telling males from females. This was first noted by Peter Dodson, who conducted a study of the growth of *Protoceratops*. This is the only ceratopsian for which there exists a complete sequence of skeletons from hatchling to adult. Dodson noted that the frill began to change when the animal was about to reach full adult size, the time of sexual maturity. He showed that the size and showiness of the frill probably distinguished males from females. Adult specimens of *Protoceratops* can be divided into two groups based on the size and shape of the frill. He felt that the dinosaurs with the larger frills were the males.[12]

Chasmosaurus

A study of adult *Chasmosaurus* specimens suggests that the size and curve of the brow horn might have distinguished males from females. In this case, the males had the longer and straighter horns, while the horns of females were curved.[13] This may also have been the case with *Triceratops*, although not all paleontologists agree with this hypothesis.[14]

CHAPTER 6

EGGS AND BABIES

Dinosaurs hatched from eggs, like their bird descendants and most known reptiles. More than 230 dinosaur egg sites have been discovered, and three-quarters of these are from North America and Asia.[1] Most that have been found date from the Late Cretaceous Period.

When the first *Protoceratops* specimens were discovered in Mongolia during the 1920s by the American Museum of Natural History, they were found near an abundance of dinosaur egg nests. Specimens of the dinosaur were found in all age groups, including some that apparently had only recently hatched. For nearly seventy years, it was believed that the eggs found in the area were those of *Protoceratops*. However, when the same museum recently found more of the same kinds of eggs in Mongolia, one egg contained an exquisitely preserved embryo of an unhatched dinosaur. To everyone's surprise, the dinosaur inside was not *Protoceratops* after all, but *Oviraptor*, a predatory dinosaur from the same time and region. Such is the colorful and often unpredictable history of fossil dinosaur eggs. This discovery lent a ring of truth to the adage that a paleontologist should never count his eggs before he has seen an embryo inside. Without an embryo, there's no telling which kind of dinosaur laid the egg.

Ceratopsian embryos have not yet been found inside unbroken fossil eggs, but scientists have come close. The skeletons of hatchling or embryonic ceratopsians have been found among crushed and scattered egg fragments in Asia. Paleontologist Mark Norell of the American Museum of Natural History confirms that such a find exists for *Protoceratops*. However, scientists' efforts to find an intact egg with a ceratopsian embryo inside have thus far been unsuccessful.[2]

Hatchlings and associated egg fragments have also been reported with the American ceratopsid *Brachyceratops* ("short-horned face")[3] and baby specimens of *Psittacosaurus* have been discovered in eastern Asia.[4]

Finding specimens of baby *Protoceratops* was one of the highlights of the Mongolian expeditions of the 1920s by the American Museum of Natural History. The discovery of a remarkable series of skeletons of this animal, from hatchling to adult, is one of the most complete growth series ever discovered for any kind of dinosaur. The smallest specimens, barely out of the egg, show a remarkable resemblance to their parents except for the frill. The smallest skulls were only about 4 inches (9 centimeters) long. The frill was but a ridge along the back of the neck until the dinosaur reached its "adolescent" years.[5]

Another remarkable *Protoceratops* discovery was recently made in Mongolia. A close-knit group of 15 *Protoceratops* hatchlings were collected in what appears to be a bowl-shaped nest. All of the babies were huddled together at one end of the nest, facing in the same direction and even piling up on one another. This led scientists to think that the tiny dinosaurs perished while trying to protect themselves from a sandstorm.[6]

The even tinier skeletons of baby psittacosaurs went unnoticed for many years in the storage rooms of the American Museum of Natural History. There they were left unstudied for nearly sixty years until paleontologist Walter Coombs, Jr., "rediscovered" them in 1982. Also from Eastern Asia, the tiny skulls and partial skeletons represent *Psittacosaurus* hatchlings. The skulls measured only 1.1 to 1.6 inches (2.8 to 4.1 centimeters) long. The total body length of these hatchlings was only about 10 to 16 inches (25 to 41 centimeters).[7]

CHAPTER 7

FEEDING HABITS AND ADAPTATIONS

Like the duck-billed dinosaurs, the latter ceratopsians developed some of the most advanced sets of teeth ever seen in plant-eating animals. They were the Veg-O-Matics of the Late Cretaceous, capable of slicing and dicing the toughest and most fibrous of plants. Ceratopsians were marvelous chewing machines.

What Did They Eat?

The ceratopsians were all low-browsing animals, picking plants from ground cover and bushes. They ate below the line of plants normally consumed by the taller, two-legged plant eaters. They probably plowed into the vegetation with their sharp beaks, snipping off branches and twigs with a snap of the jaws and a sideways pull of the head.

The earliest ceratopsians, the psittacosaurs and protoceratopsids, had cutting teeth that were individually spaced in short rows in the cheek area of their mouths. These kinds of teeth allowed them to snip and grind food before they swallowed it.

As mentioned earlier, ceratopsids had many spare teeth in reserve, as many as a total of 600 teeth in their jaws at any given time. The teeth were closely packed and provided an extensive cutting surface. But the tops of the teeth were nothing like those of the duckbills and other ornithopods. They were designed with a sharp ridge rather than a flat grinding surface. They were not used to pulverize the food but acted more like scissors, shearing off plant material into sizable chunks before the animal would swallow it.[1] They could not be used to chew or grind the plants as one might expect of a plant eater.

The success of these animals has often led to the conclusion that they were adapted to consume the toughest kinds of plant material that other dinosaurs might not find so appetizing. Their diet may have included, for example, the stringy and fibrous fronds of palms and cycads. However, both of these kinds of plants are not found much in the fossil deposits where horned dinosaurs have been discovered. It is more likely that they fed on the leaves and twigs of a new form of plant that was emerging during their time—the angiosperms, also known as the flowering plants and trees.[2]

Ceratopsians were highly successful animals. They represent one-quarter of the dinosaur specimens discovered that lived during the last part of the Cretaceous Period.[3] Together with the ornithopods, they displaced sauropods as the Northern

The horned dinosaurs, including *Einiosaurus*, picked plants from ground cover and bushes.

Hemisphere's dominant plant eaters, probably because they were better adapted for browsing and chewing the angiosperms. The fossil record indicates that the sauropods disappeared as the angiosperms rose. At the same time, as if to fill a plant-eating gap in the ecology of the planet, the ceratopsians, duckbills, and other plant-eating dinosaurs rose to dominate the world of herbivorous animals.

The evolution of ceratopsian jaws and teeth was explored in Chapter 4. How ceratopsians digested their food is also of interest. Modern reptiles, none of which chew their food before swallowing it, digest the contents of their stomach slowly. It appears that the ceratopsians were somewhat similar. Even the later horned dinosaurs, with their extensive sets of

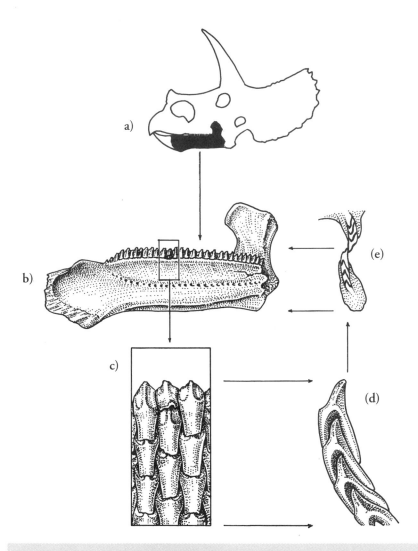

The tooth arrangement in the lower jaw of *Triceratops*. a) *Triceratops* skull.
b) An enlargement of the inside of the right hand jaw (which would be next
to the tongue) is shown. c) An enlarged section of jaw with the outer bone
removed reveals three columns of teeth. d) One tooth column is rotated from
side view to front view. e) The previous column of teeth is shown placed in
the lower jaw and in contact with the teeth of the upper jaw.

teeth, were unable to chew their food much before swallowing it. They must have required a powerful digestive system to process the food. From the mouth, the chewed-up vegetation would have passed into the gut of the animal, where it would have been digested and fermented to extract nutrients. Like the elephant, it is likely that a ceratopsian fully digested only about 40 or 50 percent of what it ate, the rest being too tough to process.[4]

Interestingly, there is evidence that *Psittacosaurus* may have had additional help in digesting its food. Several specimens of this dinosaur have been found with "stomach stones," or gastroliths, associated with their gut area. These small stones may have been swallowed by the dinosaur, and they would have been used in the stomach to help grind up plant material.[5] The muscles of the stomach would have rubbed the stones against plants that had been swallowed, pulverizing them.

CHAPTER 8

CERATOPSIAN DEFENSES

When it came to defending themselves, ceratopsians ranged from the strikingly vulnerable *Psittacosaurus* to the tanklike *Triceratops*. All of them probably had good eyesight and hearing to help detect the presence of natural enemies.[1] But how they dealt with these predators must have differed greatly.

Psittacosaurs lacked the obvious horns and frills of their larger relatives, the protoceratopsids and ceratopsids. They were small, delicate animals with only a hard bony cheek and a beak to use as weapons. Their adversaries were mostly small predators, and their primary hope for surviving an attack was to flee. If a predator was small and thin enough, certainly no bigger than *Psittacosaurus* itself, the plant eater's bite may have been strong enough to snap the aggressor's arm or leg bone. But only a desperate or trapped psittacosaur would have been so foolish as to engage a predator in combat.

The protoceratopsids were also menaced by small predators.

These included *Velociraptor* ("swift thief") and *Oviraptor* ("egg thief"), both being lighter but otherwise not much different in size than *Protoceratops* itself. In this case, the head of an adult protoceratopsid was well protected by a neck frill, a sharp beak, and a bony ridge beginning at the nose and going up the middle of the head. It was a small dinosaur but still heavier than some of its more common meat-eating enemies. *Protoceratops* may have often prevailed in its ancient version of championship wrestling.

There is a remarkable fossil specimen known as the fighting dinosaurs that opens a window onto the world of *Protoceratops*. Discovered in Mongolia in 1972, this spectacular find reveals an adult *Protoceratops* and a *Velociraptor* locked in mortal combat at the moment of death. They were probably buried alive by a sudden and violent sandstorm, entangling them forever—but not before the left arm of the predator was firmly clenched in the jaws of the struggling *Protoceratops*.[2] The value of this specimen is immeasurable. It not only confirms the predator-to-prey relationship between these two animals, but it offers a glimpse at the kind of life-and-death struggle that probably took place every day in the wide expanses of ancient eastern Asia.

Horns Aplenty–Defense Against the Tyrant Lizard King

The North American horned dinosaurs of the very latest Cretaceous Period were faced with the daunting task of defending themselves against some of the largest predators

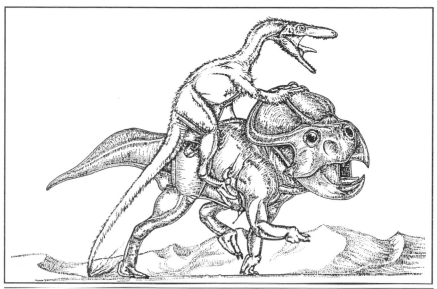

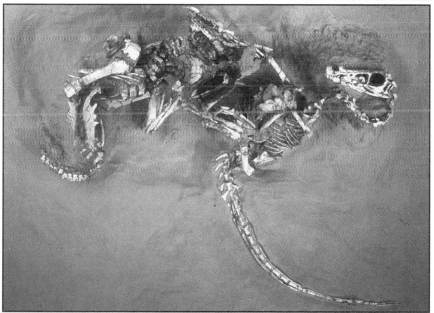

One of the most unusual of all dinosaur fossils (bottom) captures a fight to the death between *Protoceratops* and the meat eater *Velociraptor*, as seen from overhead.

that ever walked the earth. *Tyrannosaurus, Daspletosaurus* ("frightful lizard"), and *Albertosaurus* ("Alberta lizard") all lived during the time of the horned dinosaurs.

Tyrannosaurus

How did a ceratopsid dinosaur face off with predators that ranged from 30 to 40 feet (9 to 12 meters) long and weighed from 3 to 7 tons? Weighing between 3 and 8.5 tons, some ceratopsians were equal in bulk to the giant predators that may have assailed them.[3] Being firmly grounded on four powerful legs would have made large horned dinosaurs the ultimate immovable objects. One might even see that the bent front legs that made them less able runners gave them more stability when they stood firm.

Then there were the horns. As noted earlier, the short-frilled and somewhat smaller ceratopsids had long nasal horns. The long-frilled members of the family had long brow horns. In both cases, the horns were probably sharp and extremely effective when used as lances to puncture their attackers.

No matter how many purposes scientists can think of for the frills of horned dinosaurs, there is agreement that defense was one of them. Not all of the frills were bony and hard. In fact, most were mere frames of bone with skin and muscle stretched over them. But they covered the vulnerable neck area and must have withstood attack fairly well. The fossil record does not include a host of horned dinosaur specimens with broken or damaged frills, so it seems reasonable to assume that they served their purpose well.

One important question worth asking is why would a predator attack such a well-armored and dangerous creature as a fully grown horned dinosaur? They probably did not. *T. rex* would have been better off picking on the young, sick, and infirm, or chasing down duck-billed dinosaurs. *Triceratops* was probably the worst guest ever to have for dinner.

There is evidence among the chasmosaurines that they sometimes fought each other. A number of specimens have been found with puncture wounds on the sides of the frills that were most likely caused by the horn of an opponent. These were most likely rival males fighting for leadership of the herd or competing for a female.

Safety in Numbers

The social nature of some kinds of ceratopsians strongly suggests that they also protected themselves by staying in close-knit herds or groups. Although trackway evidence is not widespread for them, there is abundant evidence that the short- and long-frilled horned dinosaurs traveled in large groups or herds. Extensive bone beds, often with a jumble of 100 or more skeletons of juveniles and adults, have been found for *Anchiceratops*, *Chasmosaurus*, *Centrosaurus*, *Pachyrhinosaurus*, and *Styracosaurus* among others. This suggests that ceratopsids gathered in large herds.[4]

An extensive bone bed of *Centrosaurus* was discovered in 1977 in Dinosaur Provincial Park

Centrosaurus

The aftermath of a river flooding event in Dinosaur Provincial Park, Alberta, Canada, left a number of migrating *Centrosaurus* individuals drowned. As the carcasses lay along the shoreline, both *Albertosaurus* and crocodiles were attracted to the potential feast.

in Alberta, Canada. The bone bed includes the remains of 300 to 400 individuals, young and old. It is believed that the centrosaurs were once part of a great herd that had tried to cross a flood-swollen river. Many of them drowned in the crossing. Their bodies were washed downstream and accumulated along the riverbed, where they eventually became fossilized. The presence of meat eaters' teeth at the site suggests that scavenging predatory dinosaurs picked over the bodies before they were buried. The entire herd was probably much larger than 400 individuals—perhaps in the thousands.[5] Herds of this size would have quickly stripped the local environment of available food, so it is likely that they traveled regularly, perhaps along annual migratory routes to and from nesting grounds yet to be discovered.

Traveling together like this implies that the dinosaurs interacted and communicated in ways that would increase their chances for survival. Their distinctive frills and horns were most certainly important signaling devices. Shaking the head or pointing toward danger could have been easily detected by other members of a herd, even at a good distance.

CHAPTER 9

EXTINCTION OF THE DINOSAURS

Except for the survival of birds, the last of the dinosaurs became extinct 65 million years ago. The horned dinosaurs were among the last to go. However, dinosaurs did not disappear because they were failures. Dinosaurs were one of the most successful forms of life ever to inhabit our planet. They ruled the earth for 160 million years. Humans have been around for only 250,000 years, and even our remote (hominid) ancestors have been around for only about 4 million years.

Extinction is the irreversible elimination of an entire species of plant or animal. Once it occurs, there is no turning back. It is also a natural process. More than 99 percent of all the species of organisms that have ever lived are now extinct.[1]

Although the dinosaurs existed for so many millions of years, most species existed for only a few million years at a time, until they became extinct or were replaced by "improved" versions that had adapted to changes in the environment. To say that all the dinosaurs became extinct at the end of the Cretaceous Period is incorrect—most kinds of dinosaurs had already come and gone by then. There is no denying, though, that a mass extinction occurred at the end of the Cretaceous that wiped out about 65 to 70 percent of all animal life.[2] Even those groups of animals that survived, including frogs, lizards, turtles, salamanders, birds, insects, fish, crocodiles, alligators, and mammals, lost great numbers of their species.

Chief among the causes of animal extinction are environmental changes that affect their food supply or body chemistry (such as extreme temperatures), disease, and natural disasters (such as volcanic eruptions, earthquakes, and the changing surface of the earth). Extensive hunting by natural enemies may also contribute to extinction. Humankind, for example, has hunted many animals such as the buffalo to extinction or near extinction.

Why did the last of the dinosaurs become extinct? This is a great mystery of science.

The death of the dinosaurs is difficult to explain because they were part of a strangely selective extinction event. Any suitable explanation must account for the disappearance of dinosaurs as well as flying reptiles, reptiles that swam in the oceans, ammonites, and other sea creatures, including some types of clams, mollusks, and plankton. It must also explain why so many other types of animals continued to thrive after that event.

Theories of Dinosaur Extinction

THEORY	TYPE OF THEORY	PROBLEMS WITH THE THEORY
The Big Rumble Smoke and dust spewed by mass volcanic eruptions shrouded the earth in darkness, killing plants, poisoning the air and water, and causing the climate to cool.	Gradual	Does not explain why other land- and ocean-dwelling animals survived.
Shifting Continents Planetary cooling caused by shifting continents and changes to the earth's oceans. Water between the land masses would have cooled the air and caused wind.	Gradual	This happened very slowly. Why couldn't dinosaurs and marine reptiles have adapted to the climate change or moved to warmer climates?
Pesky Mammals New mammals stole and ate dinosaur eggs.	Gradual	Does not explain why some sea life became extinct or why other egg-laying land animals such as snakes and lizards survived. Also, small mammals coexisted with dinosaurs for many millions of year without this happening.
Flower Poisoning Flowers first appeared during the Cretaceous Period. Were dinosaurs unable to adapt to the chemical makeup of this new source of food?	Gradual	Plant-eating dinosaurs actually increased in diversity and numbers during the rise of the flowering plants.
Bombardment from Space Impact by an asteroid or comet shrouded the earth in darkness from debris thrown into the atmosphere and may have poisoned the air. Plants died and the climate cooled.	Sudden	Does not explain the survival of some land reptiles, mammals, birds, amphibians, and plants, or why certain ocean life perished but not others.
Supernova Explosion of a nearby star bathed the earth in deadly cosmic rays.	Sudden	Why did some life-forms die and not others?

Theories

Paleontologists disagree on the causes of dinosaur extinction and the length of time it took for this mass dying to occur. There are many theories about what happened. They come in two basic varieties: gradual causes and sudden causes.

Gradual causes would have required millions of years of change. Some possible gradual causes include global climate changes (warming or cooling), volcanic action, shifting continents, overpopulation, poisoning by flowering plants, and the rise of egg-stealing mammals.

Sudden or catastrophic causes would have taken no longer than a few years to wipe out the dinosaurs. Popular theories for a rapid extinction include disease and the collision of the earth with an asteroid or comet.

So far, no single extinction theory can fully explain the great dying at the end of the age of dinosaurs. Evidence has been mounting in favor of the asteroid theory. But a collision with an asteroid may have been only the final blow in a gradual extinction that had been growing for many years. The asteroid theory also fails to explain why the extinction was so selective. Why did marine reptiles die but most fish survive? Why did dinosaurs of all sizes disappear but birds continue to thrive? There are still many questions to answer before scientists fully understand this great mystery.

CHAPTER 10

MAJOR DISCOVERIES OF HORNED DINOSAURS

This chapter summarizes the major discoveries of the horned dinosaurs collectively known as the ceratopsians. It chronicles the most important and complete specimens of horned dinosaurs that have been discovered, when and where they were found, and the people who identified them.

◆◆◆

1824 (England)—Professor **William Buckland** wrote the first scientific description of a dinosaur when he wrote about the carnivore *Megalosaurus* ("great lizard").

1842 (England)—British anatomist **Richard Owen**, having recognized the differences between *Iguanodon, Megalosaurus,* and other large, extinct saurians described by that time, created the term *Dinosauria* ("terrible lizards") as a means for scientifically classifying the unique animals. This is the origin of the word *dinosaur.*

✦✦✦

1876 (United States)—*Monoclonius* was the first horned dinosaur named, but its discoverer, **Edward Drinker Cope**, had no clear idea that he had found an entirely new family of dinosaurs. This was despite the fact that the fragmentary fossils he collected included evidence of a horn. We can understand how he made this mistake, however, for nobody had ever seen a creature such as *Monoclonius* before. It would take the discovery of a splendid *Triceratops* skull some thirteen years later to clearly picture what these animals were like. Discovered in Montana, *Monoclonius* was a short-frilled ceratopsid.

✦✦✦

1889 (United States)—The discovery of the first truly distinguishable horned dinosaur had a shaky start. Professor **Othniel Charles Marsh** of Yale University had been sent an extremely large pair of horns in 1887 and mistook them for belonging to an ancient bison. He corrected his own error two years later after acquiring an excellent skull of the same kind of animal from Wyoming. This turned out to be *Triceratops,* the most famous of all horned dinosaurs. Marsh enthusiastically named as many as nine separate species of *Triceratops* over the years, all of which are now considered to be just one.

✦✦✦

1891 (United States)—*Torosaurus*, the two-horned relative of *Triceratops*, was discovered in Wyoming and named by **Othniel Charles Marsh**. After *Triceratops*, it is the largest of the horned dinosaurs at 25 feet (7.6 meters) long. Its skull, measuring about 7.3 feet (2.2 meters) from the tip of the snout to the top of the neck frill, is the largest of any known land animal. An even larger skull of this animal, measuring 9 feet (2.7 meters) long, is reported from the Museum of the Rockies in Montana but had not been formally described as of this writing.

✦✦✦

1904 (Canada)—*Centrosaurus*, a 17-foot- (6.1-meter-) long short-frilled ceratopsian, had a long horn on its nose and two small horns above its eyes. It was described by **Lawrence Lambe** and hails from Alberta, Canada, where at least fifteen adult skeletons have been found, in addition to bone beds containing the accumulated remains of many individuals.

✦✦✦

1913 (Canada)—*Styracosaurus*, described by **Lawrence Lambe**, is another Canadian ceratopsid known from an abundance of skeletons. It is distinguished by its fanlike array of six spikes protruding from the edge of its neck frill.

Styracosaurus

Centrosaurus was discovered in 1904.

1914 (**Canada**)—The first recognized skeleton of *Chasmosaurus*, a long-frilled horned ceratopsian, was described by **Lawrence Lambe** of the National Museum of Canada. Discovered in Alberta, Canada, the frills of this dinosaur were broad and had large openings—chasms—in them, making the skull lighter.

Chasmosaurus

◆◆◆

1914 (**Canada**)—*Leptoceratops* was a hornless ceratopsian like its relative *Protoceratops* in Asia. It was small, measuring only about 9 feet (2.7 meters) long. It had many primitive features for a ceratopsian but lived in the Late Cretaceous with the gigantic and more advanced *Triceratops*. It was discovered and first described by **Barnum Brown**.

◆◆◆

1914 (**United States**)—Five juvenile specimens of *Brachyceratops* were named by **Charles Gilmore**. They seemed small by comparison to giants such as *Triceratops* but showed clear evidence of not being fully grown. Partial skulls were found for each individual.

◆◆◆

1923 (**United States**)—*Pentaceratops* was named by **Henry Fairfield Osborn**. It is one of the rarest of horned dinosaurs and one of the largest. It sported a nasal horn, two brow horns, and two small horns sprouting from its cheekbones. Eight complete or partial skulls, one complete skeleton, and several partial skeletons make up all that has been discovered of this dinosaur. It was discovered in New Mexico.

1923 (Mongolia)—*Protoceratops* is one of the best-known specimens of horned dinosaurs. It is one of the more primitive members of the group and does not actually have horns.

Specimens have been found for the entire growth series of this dinosaur, from hatchling to adult. It has also been associated with

Protoceratops

the first dinosaur eggs discovered, although it is now believed that the eggs actually belonged to another dinosaur, the meat eater *Oviraptor*. It was named by **Walter Granger** and **W. K. Gregory** of The American Museum of Natural History.

1923 (Mongolia)—The first two specimens of *Psittacosaurus* were described by **Henry Fairfield Osborn** of the American Museum of Natural History. They had been found about 125 miles (200 kilometers) west of the area where *Protoceratops* had been found. The dinosaur was named after its unusual toothless beak, which reminded Osborn of a

Psittacosaurus

parrot. Over time, the remains of more than 100 individuals of this dinosaur were found throughout Mongolia and China, including about twenty relatively complete skeletons.

1950 (Canada)—*Pachyrhinosaurus* had a thick, flattened stub on its nose instead of a horn. It was about 19.5 feet (6 meters) long and had a short frill with several small hornlets. The first specimen was described by **Charles M. Sternberg**. More recently, an astounding bone bed was found in Canada that contained the jumbled remains of hundreds of these individuals of all sizes. A specimen of this dinosaur has also been recently reported from Alaska.[1]

1975 (China)—Eight Polish-Mongolian paleontological expeditions between 1961 and 1971 resulted in the discovery of three new ceratopsians. The expeditions were largely staffed by women, including **Teresa Maryanska** and **Halzka Osmólska**. They named *Bagaceratops* and *Breviceratops* in 1975. In addition, **Richen Barsbold** named *Ingenia* several years later in 1981. The expedition also uncovered an excellent specimen of *Microceratops* (now *Graciliceratops*) and the famous "fighting" dinosaurs: *Protoceratops* doing battle with *Velociraptor*.

1986 (United States)—*Avaceratops* was a small, short-frilled ceratopsid, perhaps the smallest known of this variety. It was discovered in Montana and described by **Peter Dodson**.

1995 (United States)—*Einiosaurus* was a short-frilled horned dinosaur of medium size with a unique can-opener-style nose horn. It was related to *Styracosaurus*. It was discovered in Montana and described by **Scott Sampson**.

Two *Einiosaurus* engage in a shoving match.

1995 (United States)—*Achelousaurus* (named after Achelous, a river god who lost his horns) is another short-frilled horned dinosaur from Montana. With a horny bump instead of a nose horn, it appears to be related to *Pachyrhinosaurus*. Its frill was adorned with a pair of spikes pointing to the left and right. It was described by **Scott Sampson**.

1997 (China)—*Archaeoceratops* ("ancient horned face"), dating from the Early Cretaceous Period, is one of the earliest known ceratopsians. It had a short frill and no horns on the nose or brow. The teeth of the lower jaw were unlike other horned dinosaurs and somewhat resembled those of ornithopods. It lived about 113 million years ago, roughly during the same time as *Psittacosaurus*, another early ceratopsian, and was most likely the ancestor of *Protoceratops* in Asia. It was described by **Dong Zhiming** and **Azuma Yoichi**.

◆◆◆

1998 (United States)—*Zuniceratops* ("Zuni horned face"), described by **D. G. Wolfe** and **James Kirkland**, was a primitive horned dinosaur from North America. It dates from the Late Cretaceous, but about 30 million years before *Triceratops*. It had long brow horns, a trait that had not been seen before in such an early ceratopsian. It was a small dinosaur, about the size of a calf. **Christopher Wolfe**, the ten-year-old son of **D.G. Wolfe**, participated in the discovery. The species is named after him: *Zuniceratops christopheri*.

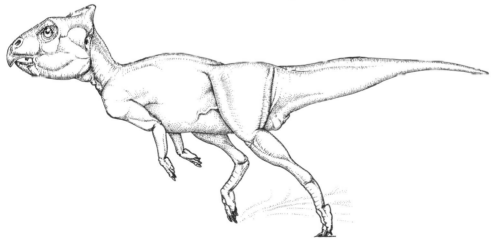

Archeoceratops was one of the earliest known ceratopsians.

1999 (China)—*Chaoyangsaurus* was named by **Zhao Xijin, Cheng Zhengwu**, and **Xu Xing**. It is a primitive ceratopsian possessing features of both the psittacosaurs and protoceratopsids and dates from the Late Jurassic.

CURRENTLY KNOWN HORNED DINOSAURS

The list below includes the genus names of currently known and scientifically accepted horned dinosaurs and others related to ceratopsians. Each genus name is followed by the name(s) of the paleontologist(s) who described it in print and the year in which it was named.

Psittacosaurs

Psittacosaurus—Osborn, 1923

Protoceratopsids

Asiaceratops—Nessov & Kaznyshkina and Nessov, Kaznyshkina, & Cherepanov, 1989

Bagaceratops—Maryanska & Osmolska, 1975

Breviceratops—Kurzanov, 1990

Graciliceratops—Sereno, 2000

Kulceratops—Nessov, 1995

Leptoceratops—Brown, 1914

Montanoceratops—Sternberg, 1951

Protoceratops—Granger & Gregory, 1923

Turanoceratops—Nessov & Kaznyshkina and Nessov, Kaznyshkina, & Cherepanov, 1989

Udanoceratops—Kurzanov, 1992

Zuniceratops—Wolfe & Kirkland, 1998

Ceratopsids

Achelousaurus—Sampson, 1995

Anchiceratops—Brown, 1914

Archaeoceratops—Dong & Azuma, 1997

Arrhinoceratops—Parks, 1925

Avaceratops—Dodson, 1986

Brachyceratops—Gilmore, 1914

Centrosaurus—Lambe, 1904

Chasmosaurus—Lambe, 1914

Einiosaurus—Sampson, 1994

Monoclonius—Cope, 1876

Pachyrhinosaurus—Sternberg, 1950

Pentaceratops—Osborn, 1923

Styracosaurus—Lambe, 1913

Torosaurus—Marsh, 1891

Triceratops—Marsh, 1889

Chapter Notes

Chapter 1. Dinosaurs Defined

1. Peter Dodson and Susan D. Dawson, "Making the Fossil Record of Dinosaurs," *Modern Geology*, vol. 16, 1991, p. 13.

Chapter 2. Origins and Evolution

1. David B. Weishampel, Peter Dodson, and Halszka Osmólska, eds., *The Dinosauria* (Berkeley, Calif.: University of California Press, 1990), p. 11.

2. Paul Sereno, "The Evolution of Dinosaurs," *Science*, June 25, 1999, vol. 284, p. 2137.

3. Ibid.

4. Personal communication with Peter Dodson, August 29, 2000.

5. James O. Farlow and Michael K. Brett-Surman, eds., *The Complete Dinosaur* (Bloomington, Ind.: Indiana University Press, 1997), p. 317.

6. Peter Dodson, *The Horned Dinosaurs* (Princeton, N.J.: Princeton University Press, 1996), p. 10.

7. Sereno, p. 2137.

Chapter 4. Anatomy

1. Stephen Jay Gould, ed., *The Book of Life* (New York: W. W. Norton & Company, 1993), pp. 67–68.

2. James O. Farlow and Michael K. Brett-Surman, eds., *The Complete Dinosaur* (Bloomington, Ind.: Indiana University Press, 1997), p. 322.

3. Charles M. Sternberg, "Integument of *Chasmosaurus belli*," Can. Field-Nat., vol. 39, pp. 108–110.

4. Peter Dodson, *The Horned Dinosaurs* (Princeton, N.J.: Princeton University Press, 1996), p. 31.

5. Ibid., p. 115.

6. Ibid., p. 263.

7. John Ostrom, "Functional Morphology and Evolution of the Ceratopsian Dinosaurs," *Evolution*, 1966, vol. 20, pp. 290–308.

8. Dodson, p. 267.

9. David B. Weishampel, Peter Dodson, and Halszka Osmólska, eds., *The Dinosauria* (Berkeley, Calif.: University of California Press, 1990), p. 618.

10. Dodson, pp. 268–269.

11. Farlow and Brett-Surman, p. 389.

12. Weishampel, Dodson, and Osmólska, p. 618.

Chapter 5. Physiology

1. Philip J. Currie and Kevin Padian, eds., *The Encyclopedia of Dinosaurs* (San Diego, Calif.: Academic Press, 1997), p. 371.

2. David E. Fastovsky and David B Weishampel, *The Evolution and Extinction of the Dinosaurs* (Cambridge, England: Cambridge University Press, 1996), p. 339.

3. Peter Dodson, *The Horned Dinosaurs* (Princeton, N.J.: Princeton University Press, 1996), pp. 16–17.

4. Erickson, G. M., and Tumanova T. A., "Growth Curve of *Psittacosaurus mongoliensis* Osborn (Ceratopsia: Psittacosauridae) Inferred from Long Bone Histology," *Zool. J. Linn. Soc.*, December 2000, vol. 130, pp. 551–566.

5. Mark A. Norell, Eugene S. Gaffney, and Lowell Dingus, *Discovering Dinosaurs in the American Museum of Natural History* (New York: Alfred A. Knopf, 1995), pp. 56–57.

6. Currie and Padian, p. 5.

7. James O. Farlow and Michael K. Brett-Surman, eds., *The Complete Dinosaur* (Bloomington, Ind.: Indiana University Press, 1997), pp. 499–501.

8. Edwin H. Colbert, R. B. Cowles, and C. M. Bogert, "Temperature Tolerances in the American Alligator and their Bearing on the Habits, Evolution, and Extinction of the Dinosaurs," *American Museum of Natural History Bulletin 86*, 1946, pp. 327–374.

9. R. McNeill Alexander, *Dynamics of Dinosaurs & Other Extinct Giants* (New York: Columbia University Press, 1989), p. 43.

10. Dodson, pp. 276–278.

11. Fastovsky and Weishampel, p. 439.

12. Peter Dodson, "Quantitative Aspects of Relative Growth and Sexual Dimorphism in *Protoceratops*," *Journal of Paleontology*, vol. 50, pp. 929–940.

13. David B. Weishampel, Peter Dodson, and Halszka Osmólska, eds., *The Dinosauria* (Berkeley, Calif.: University of California Press, 1990), p. 618.

14. Personal communication with Peter Dodson, August 29, 2000.

Chapter 6. Eggs and Babies

1. Kenneth Carpenter, *Eggs, Nests, and Baby Dinosaurs* (Bloomington, Ind.:, Indiana University Press, 1999), pp. 8–30.

2. Personal communication with Mark Norell, May 10, 2000.

3. Peter Dodson, *The Horned Dinosaurs* (Princeton, N.J.: Princeton University Press, 1996), pp. 154.

4. Kenneth Carpenter, Karl F. Hirsch, and John R. Horner, eds., *Dinosaur Eggs and Babies* (Cambridge, England: Cambridge University Press, 1994), p. 235.

5. Dodson, p. 211.

6. David B. Weishampel, David E. Fastovsky, M. Watabe, Rinchen Barsbold, Kh. Tsogtbaatar, "New Embryonic and Hatchling Dinosaur Remains from the Late Cretaceous of

Mongolia," *Journal of Vertebrate Paleontology*, vol. 20, supplement to no. 3, September 25, 2000, p. 78A.

7. Thom Holmes, *"Psittacosaurus," Dino Times*, October 1995, p. 5.

Chapter 7. Feeding Habits and Adaptations

1. David B. Weishampel, Peter Dodson, and Halszka Osmólska, eds., *The Dinosauria* (Berkeley, Calif.: University of California Press, 1990), pp. 617–618.

2. Peter Dodson, *The Horned Dinosaurs* (Princeton, N.J.: Princeton University Press, 1996), pp. 265–266.

3. Weishampel, Dodson, and Osmólska, p. 617.

4. Based on Debbie Ciszek, "Asian Elephant," *Animal Diversity Web* (University of Michigan), September 5, 1997 <http://animaldiversity.ummz.umich.edu/index.html> (February 5, 2000).

5. Philip J. Currie and Kevin Padian, eds., *The Encyclopedia of Dinosaurs* (San Diego, Calif.: Academic Press, 1997), p. 612.

Chapter 8. Ceratopsian Defenses

1. Peter Dodson, *The Horned Dinosaurs* (Princeton, N.J.: Princeton University Press, 1996), p. 19.

2. James O. Farlow and Michael K. Brett-Surman, eds., *The Complete Dinosaur* (Bloomington, Ind.: Indiana University Press, 1997), pp. 372–373.

3. Dodson, p. 15.

4. David B. Weishampel, Peter Dodson, and Halszka Osmólska, eds., *The Dinosauria* (Berkeley, Calif.: University of California Press, 1990), p. 617.

5. Thom Holmes, *"Centrosaurus," Dino Times*, February 1994, p. 5.

Chapter 9. Extinction of the Dinosaurs

1. David M. Raup, *Extinction: Bad Genes or Bad Luck* (New York: W. W. Norton, 1991), pp. 3–4.

2. Ibid., p. 71.

Chapter 10. Major Discoveries of Horned Dinosaurs

1. Peter Dodson, *The Horned Dinosaurs* (Princeton, N.J.: Princeton University Press, 1996), p. 182.

GLOSSARY

angiosperms—The flowering plants, the last of the major plant groups to evolve.

bilateral symmetry—A feature of vertebrate body design in which one side of the body is a mirror image of the other.

bipedal—Walking on two legs.

bone bed—A deposit of fossil bones of many individual creatures, jumbled and mixed together.

braincase—The internal portion of the skull that encloses and protects the brain.

brow horn—A horn above the eye.

carnivore—A meat-eating creature.

cast—To make an exact replica of the original using a mold.

centrosaurine—A short-frilled horned dinosaur.

Ceratopsia—"Horned face." The order of horned dinosaurs including the psittacosaurs, protoceratopsids, and ceratopsids.

ceratopsids—The family of ceratopsians that includes the horned dinosaurs such as *Triceratops*.

chordate—Animals with backbones, including the early backbone, called a notochord.

classification—A traditional system of classifying organisms based on their similarities in form. The hierarchy of this classification method is: Kingdom, Phylum, Class, Order, Family, Genus, Species.

Cretaceous Period—The third and final major time division—144 to 65 million years ago—of the Mesozoic Era. The end of the age of dinosaurs.

digit—A finger or toe.

ectotherm—Cold-blooded animals whose body temperature is affected by that of the surrounding environment and behavior. They may actually become warmer than the air temperature while basking in full sunlight. Modern ectotherms include most fish, reptiles, and amphibians.

endotherm—Warm-blooded animals that generate their own body heat internally. They have a constant body temperature no matter what the temperature of their surroundings. Modern endotherms include mammals, birds, and some fish.

evolution The patterns of change through time of living organisms.

extinction—The irreversible elimination of an entire species of plant or animal.

frill—A bony extension of the skull covering the neck area of protoceratopsids and ceratopsids.

growth series—A set of skeletons for a given kind of dinosaur showing various stages of growth. A growth series allows a scientist to study changes to the dinosaur as it matured and to estimate how long it took to reach adulthood.

gymnosperms—Primitive seed plants found in two groups, the conifers and the cycads.

hadrosaur—Name given collectively to all duck-billed dinosaurs.

herbivore—A plant-eating creature.

iguanodont—Any of a family of ornithopod dinosaurs, including *Iguanodon.*

Jurassic Period—The second of the three major time divisions—208 to 144 million years ago—of the Mesozoic Era.

Mesozoic Era—The time of the dinosaurs, 245 to 65 million years ago.

mosasaur—A marine reptile with a deep flat-sided tail.

nares—The openings of the nose.

nasal horn—A horn on the nose.

olfactory—Relating to the sense of smell.

optic—Relating to vision.

orbit—The eye socket.

Ornithischia—One of two groups of dinosaurs based on hip structure. Ornithischians had a hip with a backward-pointing pubis bone.

ornithopods—A group of two-footed ornithischian, plant-eating dinosaurs.

paleontologist—A scientist who studies life-forms of the geologic past, especially through the analysis of plant and animal fossils.

pelvis—The hip bones.

plesiosaur—Small to large marine reptile of the Mesozoic Era that had a squat body, paddles as limbs, and either a long neck and small head or a short neck and big head.

predator—A meat-eating creature.

protoceratopsids—"First horned face." A family of the ceratopsians including small frilled dinosaurs lacking nose and brow horns. Includes *Protoceratops*.

psittacosaurs—"Parrot lizards." A family of the ceratopsians representing the earliest members of this group. Includes *Psittacosaurus*.

pteridophytes—Early primitive plants including ferns, horsetails, and club mosses.

pterosaur—A flying reptile that lived during the Mesozoic Era.

pubis—One of the three hip bones.

quadrupedal—Walking on four legs.

Saurischia—One of two groups of dinosaurs based on hip structure. Saurischians had a hip with a forward-pointing pubis bone.

sauropod—Large plant-eating saurischian dinosaurs with long necks and long tails.

sexual dimorphism—Differences in size and shape between males and females of the same kind of animal.

theropod—Any of a group of saurischian dinosaurs, all of which ate meat and walked on two legs.

Triassic Period—The first of the three major time divisions—
245 to 208 million years ago—of the Mesozoic Era.

vertebra—A bone of the neck, spine, or tail.

vertebrate—Any animal that has a backbone (spine).

FURTHER READING

Even though there have been hundreds of books about dinosaurs published, reputable dinosaur books are hard to find. Listed here are some of the authors' favorites. They range from the examination of individual kinds of dinosaurs to several encyclopedic volumes covering a wide range of dinosaur-related topics. A number of history books are included in the list as well to help those who are interested in the lives and times of paleontologists.

Bakker, Robert T. *The Dinosaur Heresies.* New York: William Morrow and Company, 1986.
This highly entertaining and colorful account of the days and lives of dinosaurs is rich with both scientific fact and speculation. Bakker provides his own marvelous and lively illustrations.

Colbert, Edwin H. *The Great Dinosaur Hunters and Their Discoveries.* New York: Dover Publications, 1968/1984.
A classic book about the history of dinosaur discovery from the early nineteenth century to arctic explorations in the 1960s.

Dixon, Dougal, Barry Cox, R. J. G. Savage, and Brian Gardiner. *The Macmillan Illustrated Encyclopedia of Dinosaurs and Other Prehistoric Animals.* New York: Macmillan, 1988.
A comprehensive overview of dinosaurs and other fossil vertebrates with easy-reference time lines throughout.

Dodson, Peter. *The Horned Dinosaurs.* Princeton, N.J.: Princeton University Press, 1996.
A colorful review of the horned dinosaurs by the world's leading authority.

Farlow, James O., and Michael K. Brett-Surman (eds.). *The Complete Dinosaur.* Bloomington, Ind.: Indiana University Press, 1997.
A comprehensive encyclopedia arranged by topics such as the discovery of dinosaurs, the study of dinosaurs, and biology of the dinosaurs. Contributions are by leading experts in the field.

Gallagher, William B. *When Dinosaurs Roamed New Jersey.* New Brunswick, N.J.: Rutgers University Press, 1997.
Prior to the widespread discovery of dinosaurs in the North American West, New Jersey was the mecca of dinosaur science on this continent. Paleontologist William Gallagher is still searching for dinosaurs in New Jersey and provides a lively and accessible account of dinosaurs and other important fossils found in the Garden State.

Holmes, Thom. *Fossil Feud: The Rivalry of the First American Dinosaur Hunters.* Parsippany, N.J.: Julian Messner, 1998.
The true story of two rival nineteenth-century American dinosaur scientists, Edward Drinker Cope of Philadelphia and Othniel Charles Marsh of New Haven, Connecticut. Their bitter rivalry to find the most dinosaurs ignited dinosaur science in the latter half of the 1800s.

Horner, John R., and James Gorman. *Digging Dinosaurs.* New York: Workman Publishing Co., Inc., 1988.
This personal account of the discovery of duck-billed dinosaur eggs and nests by John "Jack" Horner highlights Horner's fossil evidence for dinosaur behavior.

Norell, Mark A., Eugene S. Gaffney, and Lowell Dingus. *Discovering Dinosaurs.* New York: Alfred A. Knopf, 1995.
Excellent question-and-answer book from the American Museum of Natural History in New York City, home of the world's largest collection of dinosaur fossils.

Norman, David. *The Illustrated Encyclopedia of Dinosaurs.* London: Salamander Books, 1985.
Richly illustrated and comprehensive encyclopedia for all ages.

Russell, Dale A. *The Dinosaurs of North America: An Odyssey in Time.* Minocqua, Wis.: NorthWord Press, 1989.
An elegant examination of dinosaurs and the world they lived in, richly illustrated with contemporary photographs of dinosaur fossil sites. It is one of the best books available that describes the environment of the dinosaurs.

Spalding, David A. *Dinosaur Hunters.* Rocklin, Calif.: Prima Publishing, 1993.
The history of dinosaur science as seen through the work of its most famous contributors. This book is a good complement to Colbert's The Great Dinosaur Hunters and Their Discoveries *and covers many developments since Colbert's history in 1968.*

Sternberg, Charles H. *Life of a Fossil Hunter.* New York: Dover, 1990.
A reprint of the original 1909 memoir by one of paleontology's most famous fossil collectors. Sternberg worked for both Cope and Marsh during his long and illustrious career.

Weishampel, David B., and Luther Young. *Dinosaurs of the East Coast.* Baltimore, Md.: Johns Hopkins University Press, 1996.
The history of dinosaur discovery in the eastern half of North America is explored by this fascinating book combining science, history, and the results of new research into North America's dinosaur heritage.

INTERNET ADDRESSES

American Museum of Natural History. *Fossil Halls.* n.d. <http://www.amnh.org/exhibitions/fossil_halls/index.html> (March 16, 2001).

National Geographic Society. *Dinosaur Eggs.* n.d. <http://www.nationalgeographic.com/dinoeggs/> (March 16, 2001).

The Natural History Museum, London. *Dinosaur Data Files.* n.d. <http://www.nhm.ac.uk/education/online/dinosaur_data_files.html> (March 16, 2001).

Russ Jacobson. *Dino Russ's Lair: Dinosaur and Vertebrate Paleontology Information.* n.d. <http://www.isgs.uiuc.edu/dinos/dinos_home.html> (March 16, 2001).

Scotese, Christopher R. *Paleomap Project.* <http://www.scotese.com> (March 16, 2001).

Smithsonian National Museum of Natural History. *Department of Paleobiology.* <http://www.nmnh.si.edu/paleo/index.html> (March 16, 2001).

Summer, Edward. *The Dinosaur Interplanetary Gazette.* n.d. <http://www.dinosaur.org/frontpage.html> (March 16, 2001).

Tyrrell Museum of Palaeontology, Alberta. *Dinosaur Hall.* n.d. <http://www.tyrrellmuseum.com/tour/dinohall.html> (March 16, 2001).

University of Bristol. *Dinobase.* n.d. <http://palaeo.gly. bris.ac.uk/dinobase/dinopage.html> (March 16, 2001).

University of California, Berkeley, Museum of Paleontology. *The Dinosauria: Truth Is Stranger Than Fiction.* n.d. <http://www.ucmp.berkeley.edu/diapsids/dinosaur.html> (March 16, 2001).

INDEX

A

Achelousaurus, 104
Albertosaurus, 88
Alexander, Robert McNeill, 72
American Museum of Natural History, 75–77, 102
amniotes, 27
anatomy, 41–62
Anchiceratops, 58, 64, 66, 89
angiosperms, 80–81
Archaeoceratops, 104
archosaurs, 29, 30
Arrhinoceratops, 107
Asiaceratops, 107
Avaceratops, 103

B

Bagaceratops, 107
bilateral symmetry, 42
bones, 68
Brachyceratops, 76, 101
braincase, 64, 65
brains and intelligence, 63–65
Breviceratops, 107
Brown, Barnum, 101
Buckland, William, 97

C

centrosaurines, 55, 56, 57
Centrosaurus, 24, 56, 89, 99
Ceratopsia, 31, 32, 62

ceratopsians
   anatomy, 44–45
   beak, 45, 52, 53, 85
   defenses, 34, 47, 59, 60–61, 65, 85–91
   definition, 21–22
   eating habits, 731, 9–83
   fossil evidence for, 24
   frills, 21–22, 34, 45, 46, 47, 48, 52, 53, 56, 59, 60–61, 67, 74, 76, 88, 91
   geographic range of, 24, 35–39
   kinds, 24–25, 31–34
   males and females, 52, 53, 73–74
   size, 44, 55, 57, 70, 99
ceratopsids, 22, 32, 34, 44, 47–49, 85
Chaoyangsaurus, 31–32, 106
chasmosaurines, 55, 56, 57
Chasmosaurus, 50–51, 57, 74, 89, 101
Cheng Zhengwu, 106
Coombs, Jr., Walter, 77
Cope, Edward Drinker, 98
crocodiles, 29, 65, 94

D

Daspletosaurus, 88
Diapsida, 29

digestion, 81–83
dinosaurs
    armored, 30, 42, 63
    definition, 17–19
    Dinosauria, 98
    duck-billed, 30, 42, 44, 79, 80, 81
    evolution of, 27–30
    hip, 18, 30, 32, 42–44
    metabolism, 69–71
    number of kinds, 21
Dinosaur Provincial Park (Canada), 89–90
Dodson, Peter, 72, 74, 103
Dong Zhiming, 105
dromaeosaurs, 30

E
ectotherms, 69
eggs and babies, 75–77
Einiosaurus, 57, 81, 104
endotherms, 69
evolution, 27–30
extinction, 93–96
eyesight, 66–67

F
fighting dinosaurs, 86
fossils, 19, 34, 37, 50, 64, 67, 75, 81

G
gastric fermentation, 71
geological and evolutionary time scale, 20
gigantothermy, 70–72

Gilmore, Charles, 101
Gondwana, 36
Granger, Walter, 102
Gregory, W. K., 102
growth rate, 67–69

H
homology, 42
horned dinosaurs. *See* ceratopsians.
horns, 47, 51, 55–57

I
intelligence, 63–65

K
Kirkland, James, 105
Kulceratops, 108

L
Lambe, Lawrence, 99, 101
Laurasia, 36
lepidosaurs, 29
Leptoceratops, 53, 101

M
Marsh, Othniel Charles, 98, 99
Megalosaurus, 97, 98
Microceratops, 107
migration, 36
Monoclonius, 56, 98
Montanoceratops, 107
mosasaurs, 17
Museum of the Rockies (Montana), 99

N

National Museum of Canada, 101
Neoceratopsia, 31
nerves, 65–66
Norell, Mark, 76

O

ornithischian, 30, 32, 42
ornithopods, 30, 32, 35, 52, 80
Osborn, Henry Fairfield, 101, 102
Oviraptor, 75, 86, 102
Owen, Richard, 98

P

Pachyrhinosaurus, 55, 56–57, 89, 103, 104
paleontology, 19, 21
Pangaea, 35, 36
Pentaceratops, 51, 55, 57, 72, 101
physiology, 63–74
plesiosaurs, 17
Protoceratops, 24, 31, 47, 53, 67, 68, 74, 75, 76, 86, 87, 101, 102, 105
protoceratopsids, 22, 31, 34, 44, 46, 52, 53, 54, 79, 85
psittacosaurs, 22, 31, 32, 34, 44, 45–46, 52, 69, 76, 79, 85
Psittacosaurus, 24, 31, 32, 46, 51, 54, 69, 76, 77, 83, 85, 102, 105
pterosaurs, 17, 29

R

Reptilia, 29

S

Sampson, Scott, 104
saurischian, 30, 42
sauropods, 30, 35, 42, 44, 63, 80
senses, 65–67
sexual dimorphism, 73
skin color, 51
skin, 50–51
skulls, 44, 45, 49, 51–62, 76, 77
social combat, 61
speed, 48, 72–73
stegosaurs, 30, 63
Sternberg, Charles M., 103
Styracosaurus, 55, 56, 89, 99, 104

T

teeth, 32, 34, 44, 46, 49, 52, 53, 57, 79, 80–82
thecodonts, 29
theropods, 30, 35, 42, 65
Torosaurus, 51, 55, 57, 60, 72, 99
trace fossils, 50–51
trackways, 72, 89
Triceratops, 21–22, 24–25, 47, 55, 57, 59, 62, 64, 66, 72, 74, 85, 89, 98, 99, 101, 105
Turanoceratops, 108
Tyrannosaurus, 22, 55, 59, 88, 89

U

Udanoceratops, 108

V

Velociraptor, 86, 87
vertebrates 27, 29
    definition, 41–42
    origins, 41

W

Wolfe, Christopher, 105

Wolfe, D. G., 105

X

Xu Xing, 106

Y

Yoichi, Azuma, 105

Z

Zhao Xijin, 106
Zuniceratops, 105